Prac

Publish

the Britis..

D0491038

Founding editor: Jo Campling

Social Work is a multi-skilled profession, centred on people. Social workers need skills in problem-solving, communication, critical reflection and working with others to be effective in practice.

The British Association of Social Workers (www.basw.co.uk) has always been conscious of its role in setting guidelines for practice and in seeking to raise professional standards. The concept of the Practical Social Work series was developed to fulfil a genuine professional need for a carefully planned, coherent, series of texts that would contribute to practitioners' skills, development and professionalism.

Newly relaunched to meet the ever-changing needs of the social work profession, the series has been reviewed and revised with the help of the BASW Editorial Advisory Board:

Peter Beresford
Jim Campbell
Monica Dowling
Brian Littlechild
Mark Lymbery
Fraser Mitchell
Steve Moore

Under their guidance each book marries practice issues with theory and research in a compact and applied format: perfect for students, practitioners and educators.

A comprehensive list of titles available in the series can be found online at: www.palgrave.com/socialwork/basw

Series standing order **ISBN 0–333–80313–2**

You can receive future titles in this series as they are published by placing a standing order. Please contact your bookseller or, in the case of difficulty, contact us at the address below with your name and address, the title of the series and the ISBN quoted above.

Customer Services Department, Macmillan Distribution Ltd, Houndmills, Basingstoke, Hampshire RG21 6XS, England

Practical social work series

New titles

Sarah Banks *Ethics and Values in Social Work* **(4th edition)**

Veronica Coulshed and Joan Orme *Social Work Practice* **(5th edition)**

Veronica Coulshed, Audrey Mullender and Margaret McClade *Management in Social Work* **(4th edition) Coming soon!**

Celia Doyle *Working with Abused Children* **(4th edition)**

Gordon Jack and Helen Donnellan *Social Work with Children* **Coming soon!**

Paula Nicolson and Rowan Bayne *Psychology for Social Work Theory and Practice* **(4th edition) Coming soon!**

Michael Oliver, Bob Sapey and Pamela Thomas *Social Work with Disabled People* **(4th edition)**

Mo Ray and Judith Philips *Social Work with Older People* **(5th edition)**

Steven Shardlow and Mark Doel *Practice Learning and Teaching* **(2nd edition) Coming soon!**

Neil Thompson *Anti-Discriminatory Practice* **(5th edition)**

For further companion resources visit www.palgrave.com/socialwork/basw

Michael Oliver,
Bob Sapey
and
Pam Thomas

Social Work with Disabled People

Fourth Edition

palgrave
macmillan

First edition 1983
Reprinted four times
Second edition 1998
Reprinted five times
Third edition 2006
Reprinted three times
Fourth edition 2012

Published by
PALGRAVE MACMILLAN

Palgrave Macmillan in the UK is an imprint of Macmillan Publishers Limited, registered in England, company number 785998, of Houndmills, Basingstoke, Hampshire RG21 6XS.

Palgrave Macmillan in the US is a division of St Martin's Press LLC, 175 Fifth Avenue, New York, NY 10010.

Palgrave Macmillan is the global academic imprint of the above companies and has companies and representatives throughout the world.

Palgrave® and Macmillan® are registered trademarks in the United States, the United Kingdom, Europe and other countries

ISBN 978–0–230–29795–1

This book is printed on paper suitable for recycling and made from fully managed and sustained forest sources. Logging, pulping and manufacturing processes are expected to conform to the environmental regulations of the country of origin.

A catalogue record for this book is available from the British Library.

A catalog record for this book is available from the Library of Congress.

10   9   8   7   6   5   4   3   2   1
21   20   19   18   17   16   15   14   13   12

Printed in China

Summary of Contents

Contents

Preface to the fourth edition

When the first edition of this book was published in 1983, social work appeared to be the occupational group that was best positioned within the disability industry to change its practice to the principles of the social model of disability. The first edition encouraged social workers to review the individualising and pathologising knowledge and methods that had dominated their practice and to join disabled people in challenging the political, cultural and professional barriers they faced in their everyday lives. The second and third editions were published in 1999 and 2006 respectively and in both cases they reflected that much had been added to our knowledge of disability by disabled people, but social work had generally failed to take up the challenge. Both earlier editions brought much of the context up to date, the message of the book changed little and the continued existence of a role for social work in the lives of disabled people was questioned in light of the economic and political circumstances. This important message found international favour with these editions being translated into Complex (Taiwan) and Simplified (Beijing) Chinese, Japanese and Korean.

The first edition of this book introduced the idea of the social model of disability, the first time it had been described in this way to such a wide audience. Subsequent editions, including this one, continue to use this as way of providing insight into the way in which society does not take account of people with impairments and long-term health conditions. In the twenty-first century it is fashionable in some academic and professional quarters to try to discredit the social model of disability by criticising its failure to address issues related to narratives and impairment and long-term health conditions. This perspective misses the point that the social model of disability was never meant to do that. Of course personal experiences of impairment and long-term clinical conditions are of vital importance to individuals who have to find their own ways of managing them. There is no question of the importance of the roles of medical and allied professionals in supporting individuals in managing these conditions. Narratives and issues relating to clinical conditions are about individuals not about society. Conversely the social model is not about individuals, it is about a disabling society. Discrimination and exclusion are not caused by the biology or the psychology of individuals, which applies as much when discussing disability as it does when discussing racism, sexism or transgender issues. To conflate individual conditions with a disabling society causes confusion and hinders action. At an individual level individuals do have to deal with both impairment issues and issues that are caused by a disabling society.

Disabled people who have a good understanding of the social model have been extremely concerned that an academic debate intent on discrediting the social model has the potential do undo the progress that has been made through the use of social model understanding. So this fourth edition continues to use the social model of disability and recognises that it is not a theory, nor is it just a materialism perspective, but provides insight into how to solve disabling problems including culture and attitudes.

This fourth edition is also required because of the significant advances that have been made by disabled people in changing the ideological underpinning of disability policy in the United Kingdom. We describe this in more detail in the main text but in essence it involves a cultural shift from viewing disabled people as a group deserving of welfare, to fellow citizens with full rights to participate socially, economically and politically in society. In revising this book we have had to reflect on the progress, or lack of it, that has been made by the social work profession towards working with disabled people as citizens within a social model of disability. While this might be described as disappointing there are more serious consequences. First and foremost it means that many thousands of disabled people continue to live in conditions that would not be tolerable to the social workers and their managers who are charged with administering the welfare system, and this is unacceptable. Second, so much has been achieved by the disabled people's movement in the fight to gain full civil rights, and as those changes come to fruition, it looks increasingly likely that social work, due to its failure to recognise disabled people as citizens, is moving closer to excluding itself from this area of practice.

This edition has been updated considerably; much of the old material has been replaced, taking into account the increase in opportunities for independent living, choice and control. There is also a new chapter on safeguarding with particular reference to harassment and hate crime against disabled people, an issue that has been gaining considerable attention since the third edition. There are still some older references and quotations where they continue to serve a useful purpose. Even though the language may now seem dated and inconsistent with current terminology, this literature provides the reader with a sense of the length of time over which the disabled people's movement has been fighting for changes in the welfare system and most importantly, the extent to which too little has changed within social work.

This book is not intended to be a handbook rather it is about principles that can be maintained regardless of changing current government policies. There is however, reference to policy documents when it is pertinent. The result is a book that continues to promote the potential for social work with disabled people within a social model of disability, but which also clearly states that practice within an individual model (or derivatives) is no longer viable. Occupational groups that do not change will soon find that there is no role for them as disabled people will take matters into their own hands.

We hope that the fourth edition of this book will continue to act as a resource for disabled people and social workers in the continuing struggle to create an inclusive society in which everyone is recognised and treated as a citizen of our very rich and privileged country.

PAM THOMAS
BOB SAPEY

Acknowledgements

With thanks to Baroness Surbiton, Jane Campbell, for permission to use information from the Not Dead Yet UK website and for helpful comments around assisted suicide.

Introduction: setting the scene

In the late nineteenth century the first hospital almoner was appointed from the Charity Organisation Society and it is from that role that social work with disabled people emerged. By the time World War II commenced social work had become a reserved occupation but, despite its development towards a profession – the gaining of university status for its training its proactive stance in terms of child and health care, and the influence of psychoanalysis on its practice – social work remained essentially concerned with administrating welfare on utilitarian principles. The state was concerned to ensure that welfare be distributed on the basis that it would act as a remedy to dependency rather than as a sedative. Theoretically, the role of social workers was to assess the behaviour and motivations of individuals in need, in order to determine how best to help them become self-reliant. In practice welfare agencies tended to retain control over the design and management of services as self-reliance and long-term need were seen as incompatible.

In the early 1990s this control was institutionalised as social work was extensively replaced by care management, which was dominated by notions of financial accountability and rationing of services. Sir Roy Griffiths' report *Agenda for Action*, the White Paper *Caring for People* and the subsequent legislation, the *NHS and Community Care Act, 1990*, introduced care managers into local authority social work and social services departments. Their role was to assess individual need and then purchase the social care services that were required by disabled people to meet those needs. Social service authorities would be 'enabling authorities' rather than direct providers of care. While the majority of care managers were social workers, this was not a prerequisite and many occupational therapists and home help organisers also joined them in this new role.

Within social work itself there were and are several debates – genericism versus specialism, community versus individual, material versus emotional concerns, and independent versus state-sponsored profession – but mostly these were concerned with increasing efficiency rather than questioning its role in administering welfare. While this role still prevails in local authorities, a number of new initiatives in social policies have begun to challenge the need for social work.

Traditionally, both local and national governments have constructed ideas of what welfare recipients need. This has led to the formulated response of social welfare, that is, the type of services available, and to the construction of client groups. However, throughout the past 40 years disabled people themselves have been campaigning for the right to determine what their relationship with the state should be and this includes determining the role of social work. While the exact meaning of the term 'third way' was subject to considerable debate, the 1997 Labour government did appear to support the idea of independent living that takes control of services away from the institutions of welfare and puts it into the hands of disabled people. Direct payments were extended to include all people in receipt of community care services, and the *Disability Discrimination Act 1995* was strengthened.

The new Labour modernising agenda led to considerable changes in the structure of the institutions that surround social work. The Central Council for Education and Training in Social Work (CCETSW) and the National Institute for Social Work (NISW) were disbanded and replaced by the General Social Care Council (GSCC) and their equivalents in Scotland and Wales. These were responsible for regulating standards in social work. All social workers need to be registered with their national social care council and it is an offence to use the name 'social worker' unless registered. The GSCC is itself to be disbanded and its functions taken over by the Health Professions Council, while a College of Social Work has been formed to provide a voice for social work. Other CCETSW activities were been handed to the Training Organisation for the Personal Social Services (TOPSS, now Skills for Care), in particular the setting the national occupational standards for social work.

NISW's functions have partly gone to the Electronic Library for Social Care (ELSC) and partly to the Social Care Institute for Excellence (SCIE) which is responsible for identifying and promoting effective practices within social work and social care. The appointment of Jane Campbell, the former Director of the National Centre for Independent Living (NCIL), as the first chairperson of SCIE and the inclusion of service users on the social care councils' governing bodies were indications of a new kind of commitment to involving disabled people at all levels. So what should be the relationship between social workers and their clients and indeed, what is social work?

The term 'social work' as used here refers to an organised professional activity carried out on behalf of individuals or groups of people. This activity is geared towards the provision of services on an individual, group or community basis. The adjective 'professional' implies that those who provide these services are certified as competent to do so and are financially rewarded for so doing. The provision of such services does not merely involve the matching of need with resources, but also requires professionals to work in partnership with disabled people to help them ascertain what their needs are, and to argue for adequate resources to meet those needs. The context of such activity may be a community care trust, a social services department, a hospital, residential accommodation, a voluntary organisation or any other appropriate agency. The range of methods involved will include casework, group-work and community work, and these may be applied in a variety of settings including the home, residential care, day care and sheltered accommodation.

This is obviously a very broad definition which flies in the face of the trend to restrict social work to the management of services. While there may be adequate and justifiable reasons for calls upon social work generally to narrow its base of activity, it is not appropriate in the field of disability, for it will be argued throughout this book that disability is not an individual problem. Rather, it is a social problem concerned with the effects of hostile physical and social environments upon impaired individuals, or even a societal one concerned with the way society treats this particular minority group. As such, the base for social work activity with disabled people needs to be broadened, not narrowed as has been argued for some time:

> Many disabilities are the result of social conditions and amenable to social services intervention. Medical care treatment, for example, is not going to solve the low-income, social isolation, and architectural barriers that are major for the disabled. At issue is the conflict over bureaucratic supremacy between the medical and social service parts of government. The clash involves ideological and theoretical differences concerning the nature of the problem and the response. (Albrecht and Levy, 1981: 23)

There is also the question of the relationship between theory and practice in social work. There is much disillusionment with 'ivory-tower academics' whose theorising is not based upon the realities of practice, and again, there may well be some justification for this disillusion in social work generally. The idea of social work as a practical activity is of course politically appealing and has led to the promotion of rational models of care management (Social Services Inspectorate, 1991a, 1991b), but in terms of disability this approach is not new. Hanvey (1981) and Bell and Klemz (1981) both epitomised this approach. Both saw the matching of needs and services as non-problematic: there are x number of disabling conditions brought about by y causes; there is a legal and statutory framework, disabled people have a number of needs and there are these services provided to meet them. This tradition is perpetuated in textbooks on 'social work theory', which assert the importance of methods of intervention over knowledge of social problems or of the impact of such interventions. Such approaches have been institutionalised in the competence framework of occupational standards and evidenced-based practice that dominate current social work training, but they ignore a number of crucial problems: What is 'need'? Are the services that are provided appropriate? As Sapey (2004) has argued, what is the point of developing an evidence base for practice when social workers and disabled people are yet to agree on the aims of intervention?

If only social work with disabled people were as simple as this practical approach implies – the matching of resources to needs within a legal and statutory framework. It will be argued here that the dominant view of disability as a personal tragedy or disaster is an inaccurate one and may lead to the provision of inappropriate resources. It will further be suggested that social work as an organised professional activity has either ignored disabled people or intervened on the basis of the dominant view of disability as a personal disaster.

A major theme of this book is that social work, as an organised professional activity, has given little thought to the problems of disability, and where it has it has merely reproduced traditional thinking in its application to social work practice. A second theme of this book is that much of this traditional thinking about disability is inaccurate and incorrect at least in that it is incongruent with the personal experiences of many disabled people. A third theme will be to extend more appropriate interpretations of disability and to draw out some of the implications for the practice of social work.

CHAPTER 1

Social work and disability: old and new directions

Old directions

The social work role and tasks

Prior to 1970 help for disabled people and their families was really only available through the health service or voluntary organisations. The Seebohm Report (Department of Health and Social Security, 1968), local government reorganisation and the Chronically Sick and Disabled Persons Act 1970 led to services for disabled people being established as a social services responsibility. The National Health Service and Community Care Act 1990 led to the reorganisation of adult social services, while the Children Act 1989 brought in separate provisions for disabled children.

By the mid 1980s social services were under pressure from disabled people who were dissatisfied with the inequitable distribution of services (Feidler, 1988) and their lack of autonomy as service users (Shearer, 1984). The government was concerned with the spiralling costs of welfare services for adults (Audit Commission, 1986). The Disabled Persons (Services, Consultation and Representation) Act 1986 attempted to ensure a voice for disabled people in the assessment of their needs, but was superseded by the 1990 Act which sought to control expenditure through the introduction of a quasi-market into the social welfare sector. This reinforced the role of local authorities as the assessors of need so the disabled people's movement continued to argue its case for greater control of personal assistance (Oliver and Zarb, 1992; Morris, 1993a; Zarb and Nadash, 1994). One of the results was the Community Care (Direct Payments) Act, 1996 which allowed money to be given directly to clients. Direct payments and putting the users of social services in control became a cornerstone of social care policies: 'the guiding principle of adult social services should be that they provide the support needed by someone to make the most of their capacity and potential' (Department of Health, 1998: para. 2.5).

The government (Department of Health, 1998, para. 2.11) also aimed to take action to reduce the use of institutional care through:

- better preventative services and a stronger focus on rehabilitation,
- extension of direct payments schemes,
- better support for service users who are able to work,
- improved review and follow-up to take account of people's changing needs,
- improved support for people with mental health problems, and
- more support for carers.

The publication of *A Quality Strategy for Social Care* (Department of Health, 2000) and the *Requirements for Social Work Training* (Department of Health, 2002) both emphasised the need for social workers to be skilled in working in partnership with service users. The Department of Health made funds available to help universities pay service users to be involved in social work education and bringing disabled people into the classroom as teachers. This respect for the expertise of disabled people reflects a major shift from seeing social workers as the experts.

The role of social workers may be affected by organisational developments, but in essence little has changed. Although in theory their role has over time been envisaged as quite broad including the provision of personal social work help to individuals and families, the assessment of needs, the provision of support and rehabilitation, support and training of social care staff and co-ordination of care packages (CCETSW, 1974; Stevens, 1991), in practice social workers have had a much more limited role.

There have been a number of studies which have discussed social work in relation to disabled people, but few have been complementary. Social workers have often failed to recognise the potential of working with disabled people. Priestley (2004) criticises the core role of social work as being structured to enforce dependency:

> The practice of care assessment and management is not simply a technical 'gate-keeping' mechanism – it defines disabled people's needs in a very particular way. Value-laden purchasing decisions can perpetuate the myth of 'care' over independent living by focussing resources on personal care and limited domestic chores at the expense of support for social integration. Thus, care assessments all too frequently consolidate the

social segregation of disabled people in their own homes, rather than challenging their enforced dependency. (Priestley, 2004: 259)

The managerialisation of welfare during the 1990s saw the conversion of many social work managers to the creed of quality assurance. This doctrine claims that it is of no importance as to who delivers or arranges a service so long as it is provided, but it contradicts much of the evidence from consumers of welfare (Howe, 1987; Morris, 1993a; 1993b; Willis, 1995) that the way in which social workers undertake their duties is important. Not only does this doctrine ignore the wisdom of experience of the Poor Laws, that it was necessary for the administrators of welfare to 'humanise the relationship between the poor and authority' (Albert Evans MP quoted in Silburn, 1983) if they were to overcome the stigma attached to receiving assistance from the state, it also contradicts evidence from practice. For example, Dawson (2000) found that the take up of direct payments was most affected by the attitude of social workers, a clear indication of both the positive and negative effects that approaches to professional practice can have on the lives of disabled people. The topic of direct payments is returned to in Chapter 3.

Furthermore the failure of social workers to develop an adequate theoretical and practice base for their interventions has led to criticisms, notably by disabled people themselves, who have accused social workers of ignorance about impairment and long-term illness, benefits and rights, failing to recognise the need for practical assistance as well as verbal advice and to involve disabled people in the training process. They have also expressed resentment at being treated on a less than equal basis in the professional/client relationship (Finkelstein, 1991). In addition social workers have often been reluctant to throw themselves wholeheartedly into work with this particular group.

Adults with physical impairments make up the largest group of disabled adults of working age both in terms of those who are, and those who are not, eligible for social care. Social work support and services for working age adults with physical impairments have not had the same specialist attention as adults with learning difficulties or adults experiencing mental distress. This includes specialism in career choices for social workers. In some cases social work with adults with physical and or sensory impairments may have been treated as an 'add on' to support for older people.

As a measure of social workers' disinterest, Sapey (2004) reported that in a review of papers on disability relevant to social work, only one in eight were published in social work journals while more than half were within the disability studies field which is led by disabled people.

Inappropriate teaching about disability on some training courses may mean that workers feel inadequate or incompetent when working with disabled clients. Personal fears about impairment may mean that workers are reluctant to get involved in what they perceive to be the personal and social consequences of adjusting to a human tragedy or disaster. The major criticism is, however, that social workers, like all other professionals, have largely operated with inappropriate models or theories of disability, so it is in a sense perhaps fortunate that social work intervention has been so limited. There have of course been several attempts to change this both from within and without the profession (Oliver, 1983, 1991; Holdsworth, 1991; Stevens, 1991; Middleton, 1992, 1995; Morris, 1993a; 1993b; 1997a; Swain *et al.*, 1993; Thompson, 1993; Cavet, 1999; Oliver and Sapey, 1999, 2006; Moore *et al.*, 2000; Read and Clements, 2001; Harris, 2004; Glasby and Littlechild, 2009), but there is little evidence that employers of social workers have made significant changes in the environments in which they practise. As Holdsworth (1991: 10) pointed out:

> The practice of empowerment social work can thus be seen to entail a radical shift in attitudes on the part of the social worker, and ultimately on the part of Social Services Departments and society as a whole, if continual conflict between individual social worker and employing agency is to be avoided. However, as societal and Social Services Department views are unlikely to change sufficiently rapidly, the individual social worker is likely to experience at least periodic conflict with her employing agency as she aligns herself with her client in an attempt to fulfil a jointly agreed-upon service need.

Before going on to consider an appropriate model of social work intervention, it is necessary to discuss why the current model is inappropriate; this will be referred to as the 'individual model' of disability.

New directions

The social work role and tasks

More recently the social work role continues to be envisaged as quite broad:

> The social work profession promotes social change, problem solving in human relationships and the empowerment and liberation of people to enhance well-being. Utilising theories of human behaviour and social systems, social work intervenes at the points where people interact with their environments. Principles of human rights and social justice are fundamental to social work. (General Social Care Council, 2008: 9)

The specific tasks which are undertaken by social workers vary according to the situation, but according to the General Social Care Council (2008: 16) will include helping children and adults to:

- overcome the problems of disability;
- negotiate the transition to adulthood and achieve independent living;
- access direct payments, individual budgets and other funding; and
- secure personal assistance, equipment and employment adjustments.

However, social workers are also expected to play a role in ensuring that welfare provision is both fair and sufficient by:

> helping to ensure that public resources are allocated and any charges applied fairly, and informing commissioners of any evidence that the type, scale or quality of services is not matching needs. (General Social Care Council, 2008: 16)

Laudable as these aims may be, they will fail disabled people if social workers do not first have an understanding of disability.

Explaining disability

There are three main sources upon which to draw when considering the question 'What is disability?' First there is *social consciousness* generally or culture, then there are *professional definitions* of disability and third there are *personal realities*, as articulated by disabled people themselves.

Source one: general social consciousness or cultural views of disability

The dominant view of disability is one of personal tragedy or disaster but this is not true of all societies, and some may regard impairment as a sign of being chosen or possessed. Culture, customs and beliefs change over time, and there is not always agreement about what disability actually is within the same culture:

> A class of persons grouped together under the term 'physically handicapped' is at best difficult to treat as ethnological data. Here for us is a category of persons with social liabilities peculiar to the conditions of our society. It represents no logical or medical class of symptoms. For example, carrot-colored hair is a physical feature and a handicap in certain social situations, but a person with this characteristic is not included in this class. Nor is the symptom itself the only criterion, for though the person afflicted with infantile paralysis may limp as a result of the disease and be deemed to be handicapped, yet the person with an ill-fitting shoe or a boil on his foot who also limps will be excluded.
>
> When one introduces the concepts of other cultures than our own, confusion is multiplied. Even assuming the existence of such a class in other societies, its content varies. The disfiguring scar in Dallas becomes an honorific mark in Dahomey. (Hanks and Hanks, 1980: 11)

Variations in cultural views of disability are not just a random matter. Differences may occur as a result of a number of factors such as the type of social structure, for example restricted mobility is less likely to be a problem in an agricultural society than in a hunting and gathering one. And the way production is organised also has implications.

> the speed of factory work, the enforced discipline, the time-keeping and production norms – all these were a highly unfavourable change from the slower, more self-determined and flexible methods of work into which many handicapped people had been integrated. (Ryan and Thomas, 1980: 101)

Gleeson (1999: 195), who from a social model perspective undertook an historical geographical analysis of disability, concluded that this approach 'recognises the material reality of impairment while stressing the specific ways in which this form of embodiment is socialised in different times and places'.

Thus, the social structure and values of a society are important in shaping cultural views of disability. A hierarchical structure based upon values of individual success through personal achievement, inevitably means that most disabled people will be low in the hierarchy on the basis of their reduced ability to compete on equal terms with everyone else. Societies whose central values are religious may well interpret disability as punishment for sin or possession by the devil, or conversely as a sign of being chosen by God.

These and other factors shape social attitudes to disability. The point is that the general view of disability as a personal disaster, an individual tragedy, is a culturally specific one and not necessarily the only view. Certainly the view of disability as a personal disaster is a common one in modern industrial and post-industrial societies, but there are considerable variations in professional conceptions of disability and their implications for the provision of services and for professional intervention.

Source two: current professional definitions of disability

Townsend (1979) suggested that professional definitions can be divided into five broad categories: abnormality or loss, clinical condition, functional limitation, deviance and disadvantage. These broad categories are all individual models of disability and these remain dominant today. While no single one of these is right or wrong, they are developed for specific purposes or situations, and all can be criticised on various grounds:

1. *Abnormality or loss* – this may be anatomical, physical or psychological loss, it may refer to loss of a limb or part of the nervous system or of a sense (e.g., deafness or blindness). The existence of either may not necessarily be disabling. Someone who has lost both legs may well have a very hectic social life, whereas someone else with a minor facial blemish may never go out because of fear of the reaction of others.
2. *Clinical condition* – this refers to conditions which alter or interrupt physical or psychological processes. Diagnosis is often difficult, and there has been controversy over whether certain conditions are clinical at all.
3. *Functional limitations of everyday activities* – this refers to the inability, or at least restricted ability, to perform 'normal' personal or social tasks. There are obvious difficulties in establishing objective standards against which abilities can be

measured and which take account of other factors such as age, sex and motivation. External factors are also important: a wheelchair user who lives in a house of standard design may be limited functionally, but not so if they move to a house that has been designed to take account of wheelchair users. Additionally almost everyone becomes functionally limited by the ageing process, this is normal and expected and while various professional definitions may regard many older people as disabled, it does not follow that older people themselves, or society at large, agree with this definition.

4. *Disability as deviance* – there are two separate aspects of this, first, deviation from accepted physical and health norms; and second, deviation from behaviour appropriate to the social status of particular individuals or groups. In seeing disability as deviation from particular norms, the problem arises in specifying what those norms are and who defines them. A similar problem arises with regard to deviant behaviour: Who specifies what normal and appropriate behaviours are, and with reference to what? Is it deviation from behaviour appropriate to non-disabled people, or behaviour appropriate to disabled people's normality?

5. *Disability as disadvantage* – this refers to the allocation of resources to people at specific points in the social hierarchy, and in the case of disabled people they often receive less than their non-disabled counterparts. This broadens the concept of disability considerably, for it is not just those with physical impairments who are socially disadvantaged along with those people with any of the nine protected characteristics defined in the Equality Act, 2010, and so are poorly educated people, alcoholics and one-parent families.

The 'individual model' of disability presupposes that the problems disabled people experience are a direct consequence of their impairment which leads professionals to attempt to adjust the individual to their particular disabling condition. There is likely to be a programme of re-ablement designed to return the individual to as near a normal a state as possible. In the case of physical and sensory impairment, there is psychological adjustment which helps the individual to come to terms with the physical limitations. Social work's acceptance of the dominant, individual model of disability is also bound up with the struggle for professional status and acceptance:

In a search for professional status, social work has emphasised a medical, psychotherapeutic, individualised model of work because that seemed the best way of asserting its expertise and professionalism. (Wilding, 1982: 97)

In this way of working it is assumed that disabled people have undergone a significant loss. In order to come to terms with this loss, a process of grieving or mourning will have to be worked through, in a similar manner to those who must mourn or grieve for the loss of loved ones. Only when such processes have been worked through can individuals cope with death or disability.

Such individualistic explanations can be criticised for three main reasons. First, they implicitly assume that the individual is determined by the things that happen to him or her – adjustment to impairment can only be achieved by experiencing a number of psychological mechanisms, or by working through a number of fixed stages. Second, adjustment is seen as largely an individual phenomenon, a problem for the disabled person, and as a consequence the family context and the wider social situation are neglected. Finally, such explanations fail to accord with the personal experiences of many disabled people who may not grieve or mourn or pass through a series of adjustment stages. Clark (1969: 11–12) provides this example:

The loss of sight need not and usually does not touch the core of a man's intellect and emotional being. What has changed is his relationship with the external world, a relationship with which he had grown so familiar that he scarcely thought of it.

Similarly, the meaning reconstruction approach of Neimeyer and Anderson (2002) also rejects the stages model. This approach argues that there are three important aspects to reconstructing meaning after a loss: sense making, benefit finding and identity reconstruction. The ways in which people reconstruct meaning varies according to their individual psychological dispositions, spiritual beliefs and social support systems rather than through some predetermined psychological process. The stages approach has become the dominant, individual model of disability as its theories are in accord with 'the psychological imagination'. Theorists have imagined what it would be like to become disabled, assumed that it would be a tragedy and hence decided that such an occurrence would require difficult psychological mechanisms of adjustment.

Another factor is that these explanations, being individualistic, are thereby politically convenient. When a disabled person fails to achieve the rehabilitation goals set by the professionals or persistently pesters his local social services department, she can be characterised as having problems in adhering to therapy and adjusting to her 'disability'. This conveniently leaves the existing social world unchallenged; the goals of the re-enabler remain unquestioned and the failure of the welfare department to provide the right assistance can be ignored.

The basic point remains: instead of questioning social reality with regard to disability, social workers simply proceed on the basis of taken-for-granted everyday meanings. However, as so many disabled people are able to function at a reasonable level, it is surely more logical to assume that this is a normal everyday reaction. To put the matter simply, adjustment may be normal and not a problem at all. Finkelstein has argued that the use of such concepts is nothing less than the imposition of standards of able-bodied normalcy upon the meaning of disability for disabled individuals, engendered by the 'helper/helped' relationship:

> attributing loss to disabled people is not just the whim of certain helpers. The existence of helpers/helped builds into this relationship normative assumptions. 'If they had not lost something they would not need help' goes the logic 'and since it is us, the representatives of society doing the help, it is this society which sets the norms for the problem solutions.' (1980: 12)

Despite the long-standing criticisms, it is clear that the individual model remains the dominant one with regard to disability and it has perhaps taken on the attributes of what Kuhn (1962) called a 'paradigm' – that is, a body of knowledge to which all those working in the field adhere. However, paradigms are sometimes replaced or overthrown by 'revolution' and this revolutionary process is often sparked by one or two criticisms of the existing paradigm. Only then can a new paradigm develop to replace the old. Having provided one such criticism, it is now worth considering what a new paradigm – a 'social model' of disability – might look like.

Source three: personal realities

There is a polar opposite to the concept which presents disability as a tragedy and personal disaster that was proving to be inadequate in explaining the extent of disabled people's exclusion and restrictions. Its source is from the personal realities of disabled people themselves and it was first written about by disabled people in the 1970s:

> What I want to emphasise is that until recently we have been saying that it is a physical character of a disabled person that causes his disability. This is really putting the emphasis in the wrong place. I want to add, that historically it may have been useful to do this, but that this has had certain negative consequences. Nowadays we can construct an alternative way of looking at disability, which may be more useful. This will enable us to build on what has gone before. Now, the point I am trying to make is fundamental to the reinterpretation of the problems that disabled people face. (Finkelstein, 1972: 10)

This involves nothing more or less fundamental than a switch away from focusing on the physical or mental limitations of particular individuals to the way physical structures, societal systems, culture and social environments impose limitations upon certain groups or categories of people. Shearer (1981b: 10) captured the need for this change in paradigm in her criticism of the International Year of Disabled People.

> The first official aim of the International Year of Disabled People in 1981 was 'helping disabled people in their physical and psychological adjustment to society'. The real question is a different one. How far is society willing to adjust its patterns and expectations to include its members who have disabilities, and to remove the handicaps that are now imposed on their inevitable limitations?

Adjustment then, is a problem for society, not for disabled individuals.

Others asserted that it is not just a matter of society's willingness to adjust its patterns and expectations, but one of removing the social oppression which stems from this failure to adjust. The Union of Physically Impaired Against Segregation (UPIAS) stated:

> In our view, it is society which disables physically impaired people. Disability is something imposed on top of our impairments by the way we are unnecessarily isolated and excluded from full participation in society. To understand this it is necessary to grasp the distinction between the physical impairment and the social situation, called 'disability', of people with such

impairment. Thus we define impairment as lacking part of or all of a limb, or having a defective limb, organism or mechanism of the body: and disability as the disadvantage or restriction of activity caused by a contemporary social organisation which takes no or little account of people who have physical impairments and thus excludes them in the mainstream of social activities ... disability is therefore a particular form of social oppression. (1976: 3–4)

This social model of disability acknowledges impairment as being a cause of individual limitation, but disability is imposed on top this. This may be summed up this way:

Disability is the disadvantage or restriction of activity caused by the political, economic and cultural norms of a society which takes little or no account of people who have impairments and thus excludes them from mainstream activity. (Therefore disability, like racism or sexism, is discrimination and social oppression).

Impairment is a characteristic of the mind, body or senses within an individual which is long term and may, or may not, be the result of disease, genetics or injury.

Impairment of some sort along with the personal limitations it brings is a normal and constant part of the diversity of the human species, disability is not a constant and changes according to the situation, culture and societal systems and practices. A major effect of society not taking account of people with impairments is the creation of disabling barriers; these can be attitudinal, systemic, cultural or physical. When using this social model of disability the term 'disabled people' means people with impairments who are disabled by society.

This social model of disability, like all paradigms, fundamentally affects society's world-view and within that, the way particular problems are seen. In short the individual model focuses on the functional limitations of individuals in attempting to use their own environment. The social model, however, sees disability as being created by the way the social world, for example employment, housing, leisure and health facilities, are unsuited to the needs of particular individuals.

While both Shearer and UPIAS advocated a social model of disability, Shearer is asking society (i.e., non-disabled society) to remove the disability imposed upon impaired individuals, whereas

UPIAS argue that disability will only be removed by disabled people themselves engaged in active 'struggles'. Thus, the former sees the reduction or removal of disability as something which may be given, whereas the latter sees it as having to be taken. There are different implications for professional practice stemming from these views, which are to do with whether professionals wish to be in control themselves, or to work in collaboration with disabled people.

The thinking behind the social model of disability has come from disabled people with physical impairments (Finkelstein, 1980; Shearer, 1981; UPIAS, 1976), however it is just as useful when considering the situation of people with other impairments. Harris (1995) suggests that Deaf people who use British Sign Language suffer disadvantages from linguistic isolation in employment situations where the majority of workers are hearing. Pressure is exerted upon Deaf workers to behave as much like hearing workers as possible and Harris argues that many Deaf people are left to work in situations where there is a complete lack of meaningful communication between themselves and colleagues. The disadvantages suffered by Deaf people stem from a lack of tolerance and respect by management and co-workers for linguistic difference and as such, become individualised as a problem for Deaf workers to solve, rather than for hearing people to view as a challenge (Harris, 1997). Harris suggests that such a change in attitudes by hearing people and a willingness to learn BSL could radically alter the pattern of disadvantage and provide an empowering environment for Deaf people.

Sayce (2000) and Beresford (2004) both argue that the social model of disability has relevance for people with mental distress. Sayce describes a disability-inclusion model in which she calls for a two-pronged attack on the causes of stigma and social exclusion, first strong anti-discrimination legislation and second, the assertion of a positive identity by saying 'no to shame'. Both she and Beresford also recognise that there may be tensions, not least because the social model is accepting of the notion of impairment whereas many people labelled as 'mentally ill' would not see their 'distress' as an impairment. However other may perceive them as impaired and discriminate on that basis (Beresford, 2004).

Despite the perception that the social model is reliant on accepting the concept of impairment others have criticised the use of social model for not taking enough account of impairment (Morris, 1991; Crow, 1996), this will returned to in the next chapter. The social model has also been criticised for not taking account of the use of agency (Allen *et al.*, 2002). It needs to be recognised that people do use agency in order manage their impairments and to make use of an environment, which may not be designed with them in mind. Examining the use of agency may be useful in exploring how people with impairments cope in society, in addition to examining societal systems and practices where the social model of disability is the most useful tool.

A further criticism of the social model was raised by Stuart (1994), who suggests that the social model has been used in a way that has tended to be an exclusive analysis that had failed to acknowledge the multiple oppressions of black disabled people. He explains:

> The oppression of medicalisation and the potential for empowerment of the social model is as relevant to black disabled people as it is to any other disabled people. The legitimate point of view of this group should be perceived as, perhaps, broadening our understanding of the disabling process and the methods of achieving empowerment. It should also be acknowledged that these people might not accept that the social model, as it is currently theorised, will provide the intended liberation. To do so, it is important to acknowledge that disability itself has been racialised. In other words, the perception of disability differs depending upon the colour of an individual's skin or his or her ethnic identity. (Stuart, 1994: 372)

This experience of black disabled people suggested that racism was operating within disability studies and the disabled people's movement, just as it does within other institutions in Britain and that organisations of disabled people are not in some way exempt or immune from acting oppressively towards black people. Ahmad (2000) argued that the social model may 'seem over-westernised' as it has come from a political movement that is historically and culturally specific. The use of the social model of disability needs to ensure that an ethnically diverse and multi-cultural and multi-faith approach is taken, in order to incorporate an understanding of these differing perceptions of disability if it is to provide an analysis that is inclusive.

The social model of disability is not about disabled people themselves, nor their experiences of impairment or use of agency; it is about the societal systems, structures and practices that do not take account of people with impairments. Social model discourse and the way this has been interpreted may have given the impression that the social model of disability necessarily dismisses the experience of impairment and how to manage it in various settings, but these are simply not what the model aims to explain. A model is a sort of tool, it assists us in examining situations, it may be used to understand a range of different experiences rather than necessarily dictating to disabled people what their experiences should be. Those experiences will undoubtedly be culturally located and reflect differences of class, race, gender and so forth, and so discourse may well be culturally biased.

When using the social model understanding also comes from recognising that historically experiences of disability have been culturally located in responses to impairment (Gleeson, 1999; Borsay, 2005). The social model can be used by those in different cultures and within ethnic, queer or gender studies to illustrate disability in those situations. Equally these disciplines all need to take account of disablism with their communities.

The social model of disability can be used alongside models and theories which are about individual disabled people and their experience of impairment and disablism. Drawing on Thomas' (1999) work about the psycho-emotional dimensions of disablism, Reeve (2002) discusses the way in which oppression becomes internalised for disabled people, not as a result of an individual psychological deficiency, but as a consequence of their treatment within a disabling society. The implicit values of the social model have been shown to be effective in combating these effects, for example Tate *et al.* (1992) reported on a study which showed that people with spinal injuries who were put on an 'independent living program' at the time of their acute rehabilitation, were able to adjust to their new circumstances with less negative psychological effects than those who received a more traditional, medically orientated service.

The over-riding importance of the social model of disability is that it does not locate the problem of disability with disabled people because they have 'something wrong with them' – it rejects the individual pathology model. Hence when disabled people are no longer able to perform certain tasks, the reasons and solutions are sought in examining the poor societal practices, bad design of buildings, unrealistic expectations of others, the organisation of production or an unsuitable housing environment. Only when all of these are fully inclusive should it be assumed that disability is removed and those individuals are no longer 'disabled'.

The social model and its implications for social work

There have undoubtedly been initiatives by individual social workers or departments which are not based on the individual model and which are indeed perfectly compatible with a social model of disability, but social work as a profession has not given systematic attention to developing a theoretical perspective on disability, preferring to align itself with a local authority construct of social service users. Even within the vastly growing literature on anti-discriminatory practice, there is little evidence, with the notable exception of Thompson (1993; 2001), of a sustained application of the combating disablism from a social model perspective.

Outlining a social model of disability before going on to discuss some of its implications for social work practice goes against the current conventional wisdom which suggests that theory should be practice based rather than the other way round. Nevertheless to rely on practice to inform theory when practitioners may have already internalised an inappropriate model is to perpetuate the problem, for it would merely result in reinforcement of the individual model of disability at a theoretical level. It also needs to be borne in mind that the social model of disability was developed from the real lives of disabled people – so in a sense it is from the practice of disabled people rather than social workers. From a social work perspective we will attempt to lay the theoretical base before considering some of the practice implications. This discussion will inevitably be brief; for using the social model of disability is subjective. Practitioners themselves will need to work in conjunction with their disabled clients to find the full implications; it is not for academics to extract practice blue-prints from their theories.

If consideration is first given to the three main traditional social work approaches (casework, group work and community work), it is possible to make a number of statements relevant to practice. For example, the switch from an individual to a social model of disability does not signify the death of casework. Rather, it sees casework as one of a range of options for skilled intervention. It does not deny that some people may grieve or mourn for their lost able body, but suggests that such a view should not dominate the social worker's assessment of what the problem may be. Thus, grief work or bereavement counselling may be appropriate in some instances, but it most certainly should not be at the expense of taking account of the loss of independence while identifying and removing disabling barriers. Some disabled people, particularly those with progressive diseases, may need long term support of the kind that only a casework relationship can provide, and indeed, the whole family may become the target for casework intervention (see Lenny, 1993; Oliver, 1995; Reeve 2000; 2004; Lago and Smith, 2003, for discussion of counselling). Equally, a casework approach may be used to provide support to disabled people while they are learning to use direct payments effectively.

Similarly, group work need not focus solely on the need to create a therapeutic environment in which individuals or families can come to terms with disability. Groups can also be used to pool information on particular benefits, knowledge on where and how to get particular services, and even on a self-help basis to give individuals the confidence to assert that disability does not stem from their impairments, but from the way society often excludes them from everyday life. In addition the group can be used as the major means of giving disabled people back responsibility for their own lives.

The potential for intervention using community work methods is also exciting. The commitment from the government in 2005 in the *Improving the Life Chances of Disabled People* report, that every local authority area should have a User Led Organisation (ULO) to be modelled on existing Centres for Independent Living (CILs), marked a success for disabled people who have been campaigning for this kind of support. This provides an ideal opportunity for social workers to work alongside disabled people in the co-production of support for independent living using the social model of disability. CILs and ULOs are discussed in Chapter 3.

Theory and practice

In suggesting that theory should inform practice with regard to disability rather than vice versa, a number of developments in social work practice compatible with the social model of disability have been ignored. Such theory has been developed elsewhere, notably by disabled people and their organisations and in disability studies. As a consequence theory and practice have proceeded separately and have not merged into what was earlier called a 'paradigm'.

While there is a claim that practice leads to theory there is little, if any, recognition that practice has been based on the underlying assumptions and perspectives of the individual model of disability. A useful framework for analysing the theoretical basis of services that have be used by social workers and their managers is that developed by Oliver and Bailey (2002) in a review of services in one local authority. The framework identifies three approaches to the provision of services, the humanitarian, compliance and citizenship approaches.

The humanitarian approach

Under this approach services are provided out of goodwill and the desire to help individuals and groups perceived as less fortunate. This leaves producers in control of these services and users are expected to be grateful for receiving them. The outcome of this is often that producers think they are doing a good job but users, when asked, are critical and seen as ungrateful. This may also be termed a charitable approach.

This approach is set out in summary form below.

Providers
- we know best
- individual model – whereby the disabled person is the problem
- doing clients a favour
- clients should be grateful

Disabled people
- don't like being patronised
- reject the individual model
- not valued as people
- services not reliable

Result
- conflict
- lack of trust
- inadequate services
- poor levels of satisfaction

The compliance approach

Under this approach, services are driven by government policy and legislation. Obviously the Disability Discrimination Act, 1995 was of prime importance (more recently the Equality Act, 2010 has replaced that), in respect of services to disabled people. Other legislation such as the Community Care (Direct Payments) Act, 1996, the NHS and Community Care Act, 1990 and the Chronically Sick and Disabled Act, 1970 are also of relevance. This often means that producers adopt a minimalist approach; both to the principles and practice of service delivery, and do only what is necessary to comply with the law or government regulations. Service users often feel disgruntled because they think they are being denied something they are entitled to.

Providers
- meet laws, rules and regulations
- use a check-list approach
- achieve minimum standards
- show a lack of commitment or partnership

Disabled people
- feel their rights not fully met
- going through the motions
- regard it as service rather than needs led
- believe that staff tend to own the task not the aim of the service

Result
- conflict
- denial of entitlements and expectations
- inadequate services
- poor levels of satisfaction

The citizenship approach

This approach requires disabled people to be seen as full citizens with all the rights and responsibilities that are implied.

There are three dimensions to this approach:

- disabled people are seen as contributing members of society as both workers and valued customers (users);
- disabled people are recognised as empowered individuals (voters); and
- disabled people are seen as active citizens with all that implies in terms of rights and responsibilities.

Only when all three of these dimensions are met and the relationship between providers and users of services exists as a truly harmonious one, can the following three dimensions realised:

Economic dimension
- disabled people as contributors/workers
- disabled people as customers

Political dimension
- disabled people (plus relatives and friends) as voters
- disabled people as powerful groups

Moral dimension
- disabled people are people too and have human rights

The social model and citizenship

The economic, political and moral dimensions of the social model approach requires social workers to regard disabled people as 'contributing members of society as both workers and valued customers or users'; to recognise disabled people 'as empowered individuals and voters, and a powerful, interest group'; and to see disabled people 'as active citizens with all that implies in terms of rights and responsibilities' (Oliver, 2004: 28).

Two examples of how the citizenship approach could be achieved are through:

1. increasing the accessibility of social work as an occupation for disabled people; and
2. supporting the use of direct payments and extending the principle to self-assessment of need.

The latter will be examined in Chapter 3. In relation to the former Sapey *et al.* (2004) undertook a review of research concerned with the recruitment of disabled people to social work and concluded that the most significant barrier was the attitude of those non-disabled people already employed in social work agencies, particularly social workers. This institutional disablism manifests itself through social workers as Sapey (2004: 15) identifies those social workers

> who are unable or unwilling to see disabled people as their colleagues rather than their clients. While the actual terminology may vary – consumer, service-user, patient – the sentiment is the same that disabled people are at times expected to remain in the position of being helped, rather than becoming a helper.

Social workers perhaps occupy a unique position in the welfare system in which, although employed directly or indirectly by the state to implement its welfare policies, they are also the human face of that system. They not only have to represent the welfare services, they are often the only people with whom service users have direct contact and therefore play a key role in feeding-back their needs, desires and ambitions to their agencies and the broader welfare system. This clearly requires that social workers are skilled communicators, but if they are to utilise the idea of disability as a relationship, some way of linking the individual and the social is needed.

With limited resources, pressures on time from other work, departmental management not sympathetic to this kind of work, and so on, most social workers may feel they are unlikely to have the 'luxury' of working in collaboration with disabled people and their families. Collaborative working and a properly planned long-term intervention strategy is not a luxury, but is now a requirement of the personalisation agenda. It is also economically justifiable in that planned intervention can be preventative and alleviate the need for more costly crisis intervention at some later stage.

The following chapters will not be a practical manual on 'how to do social work with disabled people within the social model of disability'. Rather, it will be an orientating perspective enabling social workers to develop their practice in conjunction and partnership with their disabled clients. The next chapter starts by considering impairment within the social model of disability.

CHAPTER OVERVIEW

- Social work has failed to develop its theory and practice to properly take account of the social model of disability even though it is almost 30 years since it was introduced in the first edition of this book.
- Social work has been unable to shake loose from the individual model embedded in social consciousness generally.
- Recently the institutional structures within which social work operates have been organised to focus on the provision of services within strict budgetary limits.
- The rhetoric of 'outcome-focussed' services has been outweighed by the instinct of organisations to ensure they are above criticism from a judicial review of their activities that would be interpreted from an individual model.

- A few years ago some of the leaders of disabled people's organisations moved into influential positions within the institutions set up to govern social work and the message of the social model started to be heard.
- The inclusion of the social model of disability in the Life Chances of Disabled People report was a landmark, but more recent emphasis on philanthropy has set this back considerably.
- The social work profession has made some attempts to join with disabled people and their organisations, but this may be due to the requirement for 'user-led involvement'.
- The rewards for social workers would arise from the enhanced professional and personal satisfaction that stems from both the increased range of tasks in which to exercise professional skills and the greater potential for achieving change.
- In working with disabled people the social work task should no longer be one of adjusting individuals to personal disasters, but rather helping them to locate the personal, social, economic and community resources to enable them to live life to the full.

Points for reflection

Exercise 1

It has been argued in this chapter that the individual model of disability has dominated social work. This is largely because it dominates the way we all think about disability and impairment. One factor in this domination is the language we use. A useful exercise therefore is to examine the language being used to describe disabled people in conversation, in newspapers or on the TV. For example; what does the term 'wheelchair-bound' mean? Why are people referred to as 'sufferers'?

- Make a list of all the words or phrases you find or have heard and decide if they are negative, positive or neutral.
- Ask yourself how they influence the way you think about disabled people.

- Ask yourself if these terms make you more or less fearful of impairment.

Exercise 2

Take the characteristics (below) of the Humanitarian and Compliance approaches to welfare attributed to providers and use them to examine the approach of a welfare agency with which you are familiar.

Humanitarian

- we know best
- individual model – whereby the disabled person is the problem
- doing clients a favour
- clients should be grateful

Compliance

- meet laws, rules and regulations
- check-list approach
- minimum standards
- lack of commitment or partnership

Discuss and decide what changes would have to be made for that agency to move to the citizenship approach.

Further resources

Barnes, C. and Oliver, M. (2012) *The Politics of Disablement*, 2nd edn (Basingstoke: Palgrave Macmillan).
An in-depth analysis of the way in which society excludes people with impairments, thus disabling them.

Thomas, C. (2007) *Sociologies of Disability and Illness – Contested Ideas in Disability Studies and Medical Sociology* (Basingstoke, Palgrave Macmillan).
An analysis of sociological explanations cutting across disability studies and medical sociology.

Centre for Disability Research, Lancaster University has, since 2003, hosted the International Disability Studies conference and many of the papers presented are available on this site: www.lancs.ac.uk/cedr

Centre for Disability Studies, University of Leeds is the first and most active research centre in the United Kingdom. Much of its work can be viewed at this site: www.leeds.ac.uk/disability-studies/

Disability Studies Archive is an ever expanding collection of hundreds of papers which are not easily available elsewhere: www.leeds.ac.uk/disability-studies/archiveuk/index.html

CHAPTER 2

Impairment, disability and research

Introduction

Chapter 1 discussed how moving on from a using a purely individual model of disability to using a social model of disability opens up a different approach to and ways of alleviating disability. However the social model has been criticised for not paying enough attention to impairment and the personal experience of functional limitation. One of the earliest criticisms came from Morris (1991), who using a feminist approach and while not dismissing the social model, pointed out its limitations and stressed the importance of taking account of personal feelings and experiences in political analyses.

Many individual disabled people continue to bear testament to the value of the social model to them personally. Crow (1996: 56) fully embraces the social model of disability:

> My life has two phases: before the social model of disability, and after it. Discovering this way of thinking about my experiences was the proverbial raft in stormy seas. It gave me an understanding of my life, shared with thousands, even millions, of other people around the world, and I clung to it.

However, she goes on to say it is not necessary useful when considering the experience of impairment and its effects and this should not be completely forgotten when using the social model:

> We need to take a fresh look at the social model of disability and learn to integrate all its complexities. It is critical that we recognise the ways in which disability and impairment work together. The social model has never suggested that disability represents the total explanation or that impairment does not count – that has simply been the impression we have given by keeping our experiences of impairment private and failing to incorporate them into our public political analysis. (Crow, 1996: 66)

The individual model of disability is still the dominant model in the United Kingdom and globally, there may have been fears on the part of those who promote the social model that discussing impairment means taking attention away from societal influences. However, there needs to be a definition and recognition of impairment because all disabled people have impairments. This chapter discusses issues of impairment and personal functional limitation.

Relevance of medical control

Taylor (1977) suggested that the individual medical model approach is entirely justified in that the major causes of impairments are diseases of various kinds. In short, most impairments are caused by disease, doctors cure diseases, and even where they cannot cure, medical intervention will often control symptoms. Therefore, doctors have an important, if not crucial, role to play. It has also been argued that these diseases are 'residual' and that their increased incidence is a result of increased life expectancy and the growing numbers of older people in the population. A consequence of this view is the assumption that these diseases are 'degenerative' and largely a product of the age structure of the population. According to Doyal (1980: 59):

> The new 'disease burden' consists largely of the so-called 'degenerative' diseases, such as cancer, heart disease, arthritis and diabetes, all of which now kill and cripple many more people than they did in the past ... In addition, of course, many more people are becoming chronically ill for longer periods in their lives than they did in the past.

The diseases causing death and impairment are very similar, but whereas Taylor sees the prospects of prevention as limited and the medical profession as the appropriate agency for dealing with the causes and consequences of such conditions, Doyal has an alternative view more in accord with Finkelstein and UPIAS' social definition of disability. It could be argued that while Finkelstein suggests that disability has social causes, Doyal sees impairment as having social causes also. This is not simply a feature of industrialised economies: Guelke (2003) for example takes a similar view in relation to the use of new technologies and their role in the cause of repetitive strain injuries.

Doyal argues that these degenerative diseases occur almost

exclusively in advanced industrial societies and regardless of their individual causes, they result from the fact that the environment to which humans are biologically adapted has changed fundamentally. The living conditions of advanced industrial societies produce diseases of 'maladaptation'. The implications of this view differ from those derived from the view of Taylor, in that if the causes of these diseases are ultimately environmental (social) rather than individual, then perhaps the medical profession is not the crucial agency that should be involved. In short, if these diseases are the consequence of a dysfunction between human beings and the environment, then it is to the material environment that programmes of treatment (or prevention) should be directed. The significance of the work of people like William Henry Duncan, the United Kingdom's first Officer for Public Health in the mid-nineteenth century, was in showing the strong link between infectious diseases with poor housing and unsanitary conditions. Understanding the importance of physical environment and hygiene has played a major role in the almost complete eradication of infectious diseases that were rife at the time of industrialisation.

Indeed, some writers, notably Illich (1975), have suggested that the disappearance of a number of diseases such as typhoid, cholera, polio and tuberculosis is solely due to changes in the material environment and the role of medicine has been irrelevant or even positively harmful. Illich (1975) developed his argument through usage of the term 'iatrogenesis', by which he means 'doctor-induced illness', which he defines as 'illness which would not have come about unless sound and professionally recommended treatment had been applied'.

Medical knowledge and the social work task

In suggesting that it is the social rather than the individual model which social workers should use, it does not follow that they should have no knowledge of medical conditions. Indeed, without such knowledge it may well be impossible to consider the personal, interpersonal or social consequences for the client concerned. Such knowledge may be acquired from other professionals or through reference books of various kinds. However, in most cases the major source of such knowledge is the disabled person. Thus, one young social worker, when allocated to work with a tetraplegic woman, approached her new client by telling her that she knew nothing about tetraplegia, but was willing to learn. They agreed to spend a complete day together from the time before the woman woke up until after she fell asleep in bed. The social worker learned more about tetraplegia from that particular experience than ever she could have done from books or other sources, and as a consequence was able to provide the client with satisfactory services.

It is important to extract other aspects from the medical facts: whether the condition is visible or non-visible, whether it is static or progressive, congenital or acquired, whether the impairment is sensory or physical, will all have important effects upon the personal, interpersonal and social consequences of particular impairments. Hicks spells this out in the case of visual impairment:

> Because of the inabilities to acquire information through sight and to make eye contact with other people, the visually handicapped, and particularly the functionally blind, may encounter relationship and sexual problems which are not common to other disabilities. These problems differ for those whose visual impairment is congenital (from birth or infancy) or adventitious (occurring after some visual concepts have been formed). They apply to initial encounters, to the range of potential partners, to sexual relationships and they have clear implications for education and counselling and for professional relationships with the client. (Cited in Brechin and Liddiard, 1981: 79)

What is being suggested, for visual impairment in particular and for all disabled people in general, is that impairment effects are more important for the social worker than to know than whether the impairment was caused by glaucoma, cataracts or retinitis pigmentosa.

Disability, then, is neither simply an individual misfortune nor a social problem; it is a relationship between the impaired individual and the restrictions imposed upon them by society. This relationship is defined by Finkelstein (cited in Brechin and Liddiard, 1981: 34): 'Society disables people with different physical impairments. The cause, then, of disability, is the social relationships which take little or no account of people who have physical impairments.'

Carol Thomas (2004: 578) describes Finkelstein's understanding of disability as distinctive due to 'its *social relational* character, making it a new form of social oppression associated with the relationships, at both macro and micro social scales, between the impaired and the non-impaired'.

Identifying impairment

The distinctions between individual and social aspects of life for disabled people are important in discussing the causes of both impairment and disability. In order to understand how society creates socially imposed limitations (disability), it is important to have some understanding of limitations that are caused by medical conditions. Using an individual model of disability means not going beyond considering individual functional limitations, using the social model means understanding individual functional limitations and going further to understand socially imposed limitations.

Health and allied professionals, as well as many academics and policy makers have perpetuated confusion between sickness, ill health, impairment and disability with the words used interchangeably. Some seem to have no concept of what the social model of disability is, others cite it but go on to talk in individual model terms, while others dismiss it arguing that impairment is the cause of disability. When using the individual model disability is thought to be within individuals – so the term 'people with disabilities' is commonly used – but when the term 'disabled people' is used this also implies that people are disabled by their impairments and by social attitudes towards impairment.

Origin of impairment

There are many causes of impairment, some are an inevitable part of an individual's biology, some are purely the result of circumstances, and others are a combination of biology and circumstance, whereby some individuals are more likely than others to acquire a particular condition. Sickness, ill health and impairment are real and need to be defined even when using the social model of disability:

- *Sickness* is an acute episode causing an individual to have temporary personal functional limitation, this may or may not require medical intervention. An acute episode will pass, but occasionally may leave long-term impairment, examples include polio and meningitis.
- *Ill health* is long term, causing an individual to have long-term or permanent personal functional limitation. This may also be considered to be a type of impairment, examples include heart failure and emphysema. Some conditions may mean there are

episodes of being ill and episodes of being well, either with or without medication examples include diabetes and multiple sclerosis.

- *Impairment* is permanent and may be caused by genetics, trauma, disease or the cause may be unknown. Individuals may have ill health as indicated above. Many people with impairments do not have ill health and have had no medical intervention for years or decades, for example many people with cerebral palsy, amputations, or learning difficulties do not require further medical intervention.
- *Impairment effects* is a term introduced by Carol Thomas (1999) and is similar to individual functional limitation. Impairment effects can cause permanent individual functional limitations. This may or may not also affect the individual's appearance. Sometimes impairments may affect appearance without actual functional limitation.

Those using the individual model of disability will use the words *disability* or *disabilities* when talking about *impairment effects*, *ill health* and *impairment*. Linguistically this excludes the concept of disablism, the exclusion and discrimination experienced by people with impairments. In other contexts, say in computer technology for example, something can be disabled and then enabled. Impairment cannot be turned off and on in that way, however societal disabling barriers can be put in place (turned on) or removed (turned off).

It needs to be noted here that fDeaf people, those who are born Deaf, use sign language and are part of the Deaf community, do not identify with any of these terms, arguing that they do not have an impairment and are not disabled by being Deaf. The Deaf perspective is that their exclusion is caused by the hearing community that does not recognise their language and culture. They use a capital D to distinguish themselves from people who have become deaf later in life after they have learnt spoken language and are therefore part of the hearing community. There has been little debate about this between Deaf people, deaf people and hearing disability studies academics, professionals or disabled activists.

Personal functional limitations and disablism are experiences shared by Deaf people, deaf people and people with other impairments. Being Deaf prevents individuals from hearing and learning another language. The experience of being non-hearing is shared with deaf people, those who lose hearing later in life after they have learnt the spoken language and hearing culture. People who are deaf are not culturally Deaf and are discriminated against by the hearing community, but also they are not part of the Deaf community. Being deaf or Deaf gives rise to individual functional limitations beyond interpersonal communication, for example not hearing the approach of danger.

Classifying impairment

Disabled people are often asked by social workers and numerous other officials and researchers 'What is your disability?' The expectation is that they will answer by giving a name to their medical condition. So in answer to the question 'What is your disability?' the response is likely to be the name of a medical condition such as diabetes, cerebral palsy, brain injury, or maybe a very rare condition. These medically recognised conditions (or in some cases not recognised) may cause various impairment effects, but what these are cannot be assumed from the name of a medical condition.

Causes of impairment may not be clear cut and can be an interaction between individual, social and structural factors (Thompson, 2001). These levels interact so for example, policy at the society level may well create local NHS shortages leading to poor maternity services and a greater likelihood of children being born with cerebral palsy. This knowledge is useful for prevention, health promotion and public health, and it may be misused by politicians seeking to justify cuts to health services by blaming individuals for their own ill-health. However it is less useful to social workers once people have impairment or long-term illness, however understanding *types* of impairment gives slightly more useful information. Knowing the type of impairment a person has can give an indication of what functional limitation of impairment effect an individual may have. This can form the basis for understanding the disabling barriers that can cause discrimination and exclusion. Functional limitations directly caused by impairment, or *impairment effects* may be grouped thus:

- physical impairment (including non apparent conditions such as epilepsy or conditions related to digestion, stamina, long-term and life-limiting conditions)
- visual impairment
- deaf, hearing impairment
- mental distress

- learning difficulties (including specific learning difficulty such as dyslexia, or neuro-diversity such as Asperger's syndrome)

Some conditions cause more than one functional limitation, for example diabetes can cause physical and visual impairment, and brain injury can cause physical, sensory or behavioural impairment effects.

Prevention of disability

A major reason for considering the causes of both impairment and disability is that it raises the possibility of prevention. As Albrecht and Levy (1981: 26–7) put it:

> The major causes of mortality and morbidity today – heart disease, cancer, stroke, diabetes and accidents – can be prevented partially by changes in the environment and life-style … Disability and the costs of rehabilitation could be partially controlled if those precipitating events that are preventable were eliminated. To avoid blaming the victim, preventative efforts should be directed at the industries and governmental agencies that promote disability-causing behaviour rather than by merely faulting those individuals who become disabled.

However, the term 'prevention' as used by the medical profession is not necessarily the same thing as the concept of 'prevention' used by social workers. Leonard (1966) attempted to distinguish between three levels of intervention, which he calls primary, secondary and tertiary. For him primary intervention is aimed at preventing the causes of certain events, secondary intervention is aimed at preventing the immediate effects of events, and tertiary intervention is aimed at preventing the consequences of these events.

This perspective therefore sees the medical profession and health educators as being largely responsible for primary prevention; that is, reducing the numbers of babies with impairments being born, providing information about the prevention of accidents at work, and so on. Secondary prevention, that is, the reduction of the personal limitations that may be imposed by impairments, falls to rehabilitation or re-enablement staff in particular. Tertiary prevention, that is, the reduction of socially imposed restrictions upon impaired individuals, forms a large part of the social work task in working with disabled people. However, the example given by

Leonard of care within institutions forms one of the more obviously disabling responses of society towards people with impairments rather than a preventative one. What is preventative therefore is relative to the perspective from which the issue of disability is being analysed.

From an individual model perspective, social work has probably been involved at the primary and secondary levels also, in providing ante-natal advice to pregnant clients or working with individuals, families and communities to improve general well-being. These are also not without their problems in terms of the way Leonard sees them. It is only from an individual model analysis that assumes a eugenicist concept of 'normality' that it can be concluded for example that aborting a foetus which is impaired is preventative of disability. From a social model perspective disability is caused by the reactions of the society into which the child is born. As Dona Avery (1987) put it, when describing how she had been expected by hospital staff to follow the 5 stages of the Kubler-Ross model (Denial, Anger, Bargaining, Depression, and Acceptance):

> I have seen a 5th stage, and it is not Acceptance or Hope of a Cure. It is learning that an unborn perfect child was one conceived by society, not me, and that the actual child I *was* gifted with is perfectly fine.

Equally, the organisation of re-ablement services that focus on individual functioning can be viewed as helpful in functional terms, or it may be seen in a quite different way:

> Our first concern is that disabled people are faced with impossible social, financial, housing and environmental difficulties, and are then offered a piecemeal welfare system of professionals and services to help them adjust to and cope with their unacceptable circumstances. (Brechin and Liddiard, 1981: 2)

Social work has been concerned with the tertiary level using an individual model of disability, and intervention at this level has the best starting point for changing to work within a social model of disability.

Impairment and disability

So far this chapter has acknowledged the importance of recognising the impact of impairment on people's lives. If all disabling barriers were removed, impairment and impairment effects would remain; however there are still many disabling barriers yet official recognition of disability remains mostly confined to a model where disability is sourced at impairment. The way in which this happens is shown in the rest of the chapter, which considers official statistics that are used to inform social policy and practice.

The need to investigate disability

Good social work practice and theory requires accurate information, a key part of this information needs to come from statistical evidence of what is happening. The collection of data and production of information about how many people there are with impairments, the causes of impairment, types and levels of impairment provides an evidence base for social policy and this has an impact on the ways in which social workers operate. Policy makers and social workers also need to know how many people experience exclusion and discrimination as a result of social, economic and political, disabling barriers.

Statisticians and researchers often believe that by using recognised methods they are operating in an objective way; this belief in statistical objectivity is often shared by commissioners of research, policy makers, and the wider population. However, historically women have shown that statistics have been produced from a male perspective. Black and minority ethnic people have revealed biased research that results from the white perspective. Likewise data and statistics that are gathered and analysed from the answers to questions framed within a non-disabled perspective will produce biased findings. Statisticians and researchers have very definite perspectives – they are as subject to the collective social consciousness and cultural interpretations of disability as anyone else.

The theories that arise from these perspectives may become self-fulfilling in at least two ways. At a methodological level, having conditioned themselves in the sense that they posit adjustment to disability as a problem, researchers then ask questions relevant to that problem and get answers that are then presented as findings, valid social facts. Prior to the criticisms of this model by disabled people there had been few, if any, studies which started out with the assumption that disability was not an individual problem. The second way in which these theories may become self-fulfilling is that they may actually create the reality they purport to explain.

Research and the individual model

The psychological mechanisms and processes that research has identified and described are themselves the product of that research activity, both as a result of its methodological predispositions and the spread of this knowledge to professionals who are then able to impose this definition of reality upon their clients. This is captured by Trieschmann (1980: 47) who when writing with reference to spinal cord injury asks:

> Have professionals been describing phenomena that do not exist? Have professionals in clinical interactions placed disabled persons in a 'Catch 22' position? If you have a disability, you must have psychological problems: if you state you have no psychological problems, then this is denial and that is a psychological problem. And because this is so, have psychologists, psychiatrists, social workers and rehabilitation counsellors lost credibility with ... persons who have spinal cord injury, and rightly so?

One of the major mediums for the perpetuation of the individual interpretation of disability is through official statistics; because there is an assumption that statistics are objective it is also assumed that they must therefore give an accurate picture of situations. However, researchers and statisticians are as much subject to the dominant culture, with its individual interpretation of disability, as anyone else.

Functional definitions of disability/disability research

Registers

Attempts at counting the numbers of disabled people illustrate the long-term problems of the individual model approach. Legislative measures like the repealed Disabled Persons (Employment) Act, 1944 and the National Assistance Act, 1948 required that registers be kept, but only for those who agreed to be registered while in the jobs market or in receipt of services. Registers appear to identify only one-third of disabled people and have failed to do anything to improve their situation. In addition the underlying assumption locates the problem within the individual irrespective of their physical and social environment and fails to take into account the way these are disabling. So services are geared to the problems of individual limitations rather than to alleviating the restricting effects of these environments. Social services departments and social workers, who may have regarded registration as a crucial issue, have in fact been operating in the wrong area. From a social model of disability perspective it is the assumption that all disabled people should be identified in order to meet their needs that is false.

National surveys

The first major research programme was to the study by the Office of Population Censuses and Surveys (OPCS) (Buckle, 1971; Harris, 1971) whereby nearly a quarter of a million households were surveyed. The exercise was repeated with some methodological changes in 1986 (Martin et al., 1988) when 100,000 private households and an unstated number of communal establishments were screened. Since then most national surveys include questions which are intended to identify disabled people.

Definitions of disability in the design of questionnaires

The importance of definitions should not be underestimated; the Harris study (1971) formed the basis for much subsequent thinking about disability and played an important role in the planning and development of services. The figures produced by Harris did not prove reliable in estimating the cost of introducing new benefits, nor indeed did they always match government data collected for other purposes. According to Jaehnig (cited in Boswell and Wingrove, 1974: 449), upon the introduction of the attendance allowance it was estimated from the Harris survey that there were approximately 25,000 people entitled to it – yet in the first year alone there were more than 72,000 successful applicants. Topliss (1979: 48) pointed out that this discrepancy is 'undoubtedly due to the different definitions of disability employed', in that many people who may have few or minor functional limitations may nevertheless be severely disabled in obtaining employment.

From these early days functional definitions have come under considerable criticism, Finkelstein suggested that these definitions locate the causes of disability at the level of the individual, whereas:

Now, an alternative way of looking at this is to say that the cause of disability has got nothing to do with the physical defect of the person at all but it is related to the way that society is organised in relation to that particular physical condition. (Finkelstein, 1972: 8)

While there were very real and important criticisms of the Harris work, it did at least attempt to obtain the extent of the problems of disability in a coherent and systematic way.

The World Health Organization's (WHO) International Classification of Impairments, Disabilities and Handicaps (ICIDH) was published in 1980. Widely regarded as the most comprehensive catalogue of its kind, it was used as a basis for initiatives on disability in both the developed and developing world. The ICIDH used the individual model of disability and this informed the design of its functional assessments. These were used in studies and although there was some change in the wording of the definitions, major OPCS studies were all based on the definitions of the ICIDH (Martin *et al.*, 1988: 7):

- *Impairment:* Any loss or abnormality of psychological, physiological or anatomical structure or function.
- *Disability:* Any restriction or lack (resulting from an impairment) of ability to perform an activity in the manner or within the range considered normal for a human being.
- *Handicap:* A disadvantage for a given individual, resulting from an impairment or disability, that limits or prevents the fulfilment of a role (depending on age, sex and social and cultural factors) for that individual.

In this schema *impairment* is about parts or systems of the body that are abnormal, *disability* is about things people cannot do due to impairment (because their body or mind is abnormal) while *handicap* refers to the disadvantages people face because of their impairments or disability; so both disability and handicap are caused by impairment in this schema.

Disabled People's Organisations have long demanded the right to define the problems faced by their own members and at the inaugural meeting of Disabled People's International, a congress representing disabled people from over 50 countries, rejected the ICIDH on the grounds that it was too closely allied to medical and individual definitions of disability. The problem is more than one of accuracy as Barnes (1991: 25) states:

this approach creates artificial distinctions and barriers between disabled people and the rest of society which, at best, prolong ignorance and misunderstanding and, at worst, nourish and sustain ancient fears and prejudices.

Bury (1996) argued that this resulted in the identification of the consequences of disability, but did not result in any greater financial compensation or consideration of disabled people's views.

The ICIDH was not successful as a tool to classify disabled people and there were very few studies which have managed to operationalise it properly. Even the United Nations (Despouy, 1993) failed to make use of it. Consequently the WHO sought to revise the whole scheme and to add a fourth, environmental dimension. This resulted in the International Classification of Functioning, Disability and Health (ICF), which was endorsed by the World Health Assembly in 2001.

Through the ICF the WHO sought to create a bio-psychosocial model which they argue should incorporate what is right from both the social and individual models of disability. Furthermore they sought to end the distinction that existed between illness and disability by two separate classification systems (World Health Organization, 2002). Although in the ICF, the environment is specifically included, the basic methodological approach remains one that assumes that not only can the components of each level be reduced to numbers, but so can the complex relationships between them. Hence the scientific rationality on which the individual approach is founded remains unchanged in the scheme. The ICF is proving even more difficult to operationalise than its predecessor and although it has probably provided more work for research, social and medical scientists, it has done little more to contribute to improving the lives of disabled people than the ICIDH.

The adoption of a bio-psychosocial model within many areas of medicine has been claimed to be a more holistic approach to health and disability. However, Roberts (1994) has argued that it reverses the process of holism by starting with a separated person – biological, social and psychological – examining each and then adding them together rather than starting with the whole person. Roberts (1994: 365) states that '[t]he biopsychosocial model is not holism by another name; it is an aberration of holism, which is attractive to (rehabilitative agents) physiotherapists, as it does not threaten the concept of the medical model'.

It would have been reassuring to find that by 2010 past mistakes and the advice of disabled people would have led to a vast improvement in the design of questionnaires. Regrettably that is not the case since the most recent attempts are still locked in a definition that is reducible to impairment. WHODAS2 attempts to measure the interaction between impairment and the environment, by using the bio-psychosocial model. Many saw this model as a solution to the dilemma of choosing between the individual model and social model of disability. It has been adopted by the World Health Organization (WHO) as a means of assessing levels of functioning and disability as used in the International Classification of Functioning, Disability and Health (ICF). Yet disability is still considered to an issue of health rather than societal exclusion:

> The ICF conceptualises disability as a health experience that occurs in a context, rather than as a problem that resides solely in the individual. According to the bio-psychosocial model embedded in the ICF, disability and functioning are outcomes of interactions between health conditions (diseases, disorders and injuries) and contextual factors. (Üstün *et al.*, 2010: 33)

However, these contextual issues are actually excluded by the researchers. The WHODAS questionnaire (Üstun *et al.*, 2010)

> has been designed to assess the limitations on activity and restrictions on participation experienced by an individual, irrespective of medical diagnosis. (p. 6)
>
> WHODAS2 (World Health Organization, 2010) does not currently assess environmental factors. Assessment of a respondent's functioning includes enquiries about the current environment of the respondent, but coding is based on functioning and disability, not on the environment. (p. 33)

So the World Health Organization recognises that impairment and long-term ill health can cause functional limitations, however this is termed disability and the ways in which society can impose further limitations is considered to be incidental. Individual disabled people are compared to non-disabled people, rather than their situation being compared in different situations. No account is taken that the same individual can function well in inclusive environments, while being disabled by disabling barriers in another situation. This is indicated in the glossary of terms used in WHODAS2 (Üstün *et al.*, 2010: 79–80):

Disability

An umbrella term for impairments, activity limitations and participation restrictions. Denotes the negative aspects of the interaction between an individual (with a health condition) and that individual's environmental and personal context.

Health condition

A disease that is short or long lasting; an injury (e.g., sustained in an accident); mental or emotional problems, which may range from stress due to day-to-day problems of living to more serious forms of mental illness; or problems with alcohol or drugs.

Impairment

Loss or abnormality in body structure or physiological function (including mental functions). 'Abnormality' here strictly refers to a significant variation from established statistical norms (i.e., as a deviation from a population mean within measured standard norms) and should be used only in this sense. Examples of impairments include loss of an arm or leg or loss of vision. In the case of an injury to the spine, an impairment would be the resulting paralysis.

Participation

A person's involvement in a life situation. Represents the societal perspective of functioning.

Participation restrictions

Problems an individual may experience in involvement in life situations. Determined by comparing an individual's participation to that which is expected of an individual without disability in that culture or society.

So these latest attempts do not recognise or deal with the political and economic influences which disable people with impairments and as such are unlikely to provide adequate data to inform inclusive policy making.

Questions from surveys of disabled adults

The models or definitions of disability used will determine the questions that are asked in surveys. The argument of the social model of disability is that the causal relationship begins with the way in which mainstream society oppresses and excludes people with impairments. Part of this oppression is the imposition of an understanding of disability, that it comes from individual impairment and impairment effects. The definitions used inform the design of the questions which will lead to answers that focus on impairment and impairment effects. There is no means of providing answers about socially caused limitations. In turn this means that analysis and information for policy makers and practitioners will perpetuate the individual model.

The measurement of extent of 'handicap' in the 1971 Harris study was based on a series of questions regarding people's capacity to care for themselves. The response to each question was graded according to whether the activity could be managed without difficulty, with difficulty, or only with help. Some of these functional activities were regarded as more important than others and measurements were weighted accordingly. The most important items were:

(a) getting to and using the toilet
(b) eating and drinking
(c) doing up buttons and zips

Similar preoccupations can be seen in the face-to-face interview questions from the 1986 surveys (Martin *et al.*, 1988):

- What complaint causes your difficulty in holding, gripping or turning things?
- Are your difficulties in understanding people mainly due to a hearing problem?
- Do you have a scar, blemish or deformity which limits your daily activities?
- Have you attended a special school because of a long-term health problem or disability?
- Does your health problem/disability mean that you need to live with relatives or someone else who can look after you?

Oliver (1990:7) has argued that these questions are biased and lead to individual model answers. It is fairly simple to change this by using the social model of disability; Oliver (1990) identifies some alternative questions:

- What defects in the design of everyday equipment like jars, bottles or tins causes you difficulty in holding, gripping or turning them?
- Are your difficulties in understanding people mainly due to their inabilities to communicate with you?

- Do other people's reactions to any scar, blemish or deformity you may have, limit your daily activities?
- Have you attended a special school because of your education authority's policy of sending people with your health problem or disability to such places?
- Are community services so poor that you need to rely on relatives or someone else to provide you with the right level of personal assistance?

Bury (1996) was critical of Oliver's response to the OPCS surveys and pointed out their positive role in highlighting the predominance of chronic illnesses such as arthritis and hearing loss as causes of impairment. He argues that this helps to explain not only the higher prevalence among older people, but also the gender differences and goes on to suggest that:

> no matter how justifiable the attempt is to influence the direction of the operation of welfare, and notably social security, away from medical adjudication, a full picture of disablement in contemporary populations inevitably exposes its health and illness dimensions. From the viewpoint of everyday experience, therefore, different aspects of health and welfare needs may be relevant. Moreover, these dimensions have implications for different forms of intervention on the impairment, disability and handicap continuum. (Bury, 1996: 22)

There may be some merit in knowing how many people have impairments and types of impairment people have, but it is not enough because this does not provide the information required to understand what the inequalities endured by people with impairments are, and what might be done to improve their situation:

> Poor measurement and a lack of transparency have contributed to society and governments being unable to tackle persistent inequalities and their causes. The data available on inequality are utterly inadequate in many ways, limiting people's ability to understand problems and their causes, set priorities and track progress. And even where data do exist, they are not consistently used well or published in a way that makes sense. (Philips, 2007: 9)

The importance of finding out about inequality in statistics was also noted in the report of the Equalities Review: 'Measurement of inequality will be essential in pointing to where inequality and unfairness may be occurring' (Philips, 2007: 19).

The Office for National Statistics has recognised that there needs to be a consistent approach in disability questions and tried designing a set of harmonised questions. Regrettably the lack of understanding of how the inequality of disabled people may be measured has become more entrenched as the new questions still use an individual model definition of disability. This materialised again in the 2011 National Census which is a main tool for policy makers in obtaining an understanding of the population of the whole country, and within local authority and health authority areas. Census statistics are used for 10 years and each decade questions in the census have confused health, illness and disability. The 2011 census missed the opportunity to correct this since it has a section on health and it is here that disabled people will be counted. The question on health identify people whose have acute or long-term health issues, it should not identify people with impairments who are healthy, but given the general confusion some disabled people may consider themselves to not have good health:

How is your health in general?

- very good
- good
- fair
- bad
- very bad

This next question uses the same individual, functional definition of disability that has been used before; the word disability is used when referring to impairment and it is assumed that it is the person's impairment that causes limitation in day to day activities:

Long-term illness or disability

Are your day to day activities limited because of a health problem or disability which has lasted, or is expected to last, at least 12 months. Include problems related to age.

- yes, limited a lot
- yes, limited a little
- no

This is the second census in which a there is a question to identify carers, but again the word disability is used in place of impairment; the question assumes that ill health or impairment alone without reference to barriers or lack of other support, are the reasons someone may need the help or support of another person.

Do you look after, or give any help or support to family members, friends, neighbours or others because of either:

• long-term physical or mental ill health/disability?
• problems related to old age

Do not count anything you do as part of your paid employment

• no
• yes, 1–19 hours a week
• yes, 20–49 hours a week
• yes, 50 or more hours a week

So the newest batch of statistical information does not move us on in terms of understanding the ways in which people with impairments are disabled by societal barriers.

The best information we have is based on the individual model and confusion between poor health, impairment and disability. Some basic statistics that can be used as a general guide have been published by the Office for Disability Issues (2010) using data from the Family Resource Survey. This shows that there are over 10.8 million disabled people in Britain, of these 5.1 million are over state pension age and 700,000 are children. People often have more than one functional limitation and the figures show that this includes 6.4 million people with mobility impairment, 6 million have difficulty lifting and carrying, 2.4 million have problems with physical co-ordination and 2 million have problems with communication.

It is not clear from these statistics how many people with sensory impairment (Deaf or deaf people or people with a visual impairment) there are as they are likely to be included in 'other'.

In later chapters there will be reference to other statistics and the way in which they are based on individual model definitions need to be borne in mind.

CHAPTER OVERVIEW

• When using the social model of disability social workers must also be aware of individual functional limitation and impairment effects.
• Social workers need to recognise societal disabling barriers for people with individual functional limitations and impairment effects.

- There is a potential pitfall in considering impairment to be the cause of disability without taking account of societal disabling barriers.
- The social work task is (i) to identify ways in which disability is imposed upon people with impairments with a view to remediation, and (ii) to provide a flexible and accessible service to meet such individual needs as may arise.
- It is for planners and policy makers, not social workers, to identify the likely extent of such needs.
- Central government allocates funds to local authorities on the basis of head counts, but local authorities should suggest that this is an inappropriate way to proceed, and that alternative ways of estimating and meeting needs should be explored.
- Social workers need to be alert to the impact of official research on the lives of disabled people.
- It is helpful in examining this to look at the ways in which research has been operationalised within social work.
- It was not just a matter of counting heads, but also of making provision to meet need.

Points for reflection

Exercise 1

The Deaf community have asserted that Deaf people often consider themselves as members of a linguistic minority rather than seeing themselves as disabled or impaired. However for hearing people this is usually treated as a denial of an obvious impairment.

Discuss this in a small group and in particular ask yourselves what personal or professional beliefs you would have to change in order to accept this self-definition.

How would acceptance of this self-definition change the approach social workers might take in working with Deaf people?

Exercise 2

Design two sets of five questions for a research interview, in one set use an individual model of disability in the other use the social model of disability. Consider how responses will differ and how these finding will influence recommendations.

Further resources

Illich, I. (1975) *Medical Nemesis: The Expropriation of Health* (London, Marion Boyars).

Thomas, C. (2007) *Sociologies of Disability and Illness – Contested Ideas in Disability Studies and Medical Sociology* (Basingstoke, Palgrave Macmillan).

Breakthrough UK is a disabled people's organisation which conducts social model research and consultancy (among other things): www.breakthrough-uk.co.uk/

Centre for Disability Research, Lancaster University has, since 2003, hosted the International Disability Studies conference and many of the papers presented are available on this site: www.lancs.ac.uk/cedr

Disability Studies Archive is an ever expanding collection of hundreds of papers which are not easily available elsewhere: www.leeds.ac.uk/disability-studies/archiveuk/index.html

Office for Disability Issues is a cross-government department office which, amongst other things, produces statistical research about disabled people and individual medical conditions: http://odi.dwp.gov.uk/disability-statistics-and-research/disability-facts-and-figures.php

CHAPTER 3

Relationships and families

Families and households

Using the social model of disability can bring a useful and sensitising perspective in considering the implication of disability for family life. There are three ways in which the 'disability relationship' discussed in the previous chapter is important here. To begin with, an individual with an impairment may be disabled by the way he or she is treated by the family, for example family structure and stability may be adversely affected by one of its members acquiring an impairment, or second by a child being born with an impairment. However, it is important to note that such occurrences may strengthen rather than weaken familial ties in some situations (Clarke and McKay, 2008). Finally, there is the question of the way society treats families, through social policy provision, where there is a disabled member. These themes will be interwoven in this chapter, but to begin with the family in its appropriate social context is considered.

Family structure

The family is a universal social group, which in one form or another occurs in all societies and at all times. In the United Kingdom there has been a tendency to over romanticise historical aspects of family life, seeing families in the past as much more capable of looking after their own, particularly weaker members, and coping in times of stress. Some writers have argued that the nuclear family has always been the basic family unit, while others have suggested that there is little evidence to support the notion that the family was in the past more willing and able to support other family members. The extended family living together has reduced dramatically; those that remain are for the most part in the Asian communities (Office for National Statistics, 2001). Although family size may have reduced in the past 100 years it must be remembered that there is now a better survival rate and people are living longer. The state has also taken over many of the functions the family used to fulfil.

In 2006 there were 17.1 million families in the United Kingdom, over 2 million more families in the United Kingdom than in 1971 (McConnell and Wilson, 2007: 2). However not everyone lives with their family. Many people live alone – the Office for National Statistics (2010: 15) identifies an increase in the number of one person households from 'around 1.7 million in 1961 to more than 7 million in 2009'. As people live longer it is increasingly likely that older people, especially older women, will live alone (ONS, 2009).

There have been important changes in the nature of the family and the situations in which people live to account for this, especially the numbers of people living alone, therefore a clear understanding of the concept of a 'household' is important:

Households are defined, broadly, as people who live and eat together, or people who live alone. Families are defined by marriage, civil partnership or cohabitation and, where there are children in the household, child/parent relationships. Most households consist of a single family or someone living alone ... There were 25.2 million households in Great Britain in 2009. (ONS, 2010: 14)

While the number of families has increased slightly the number of households has increased hugely. Families are included in the total number of households shown in official statistics, between 1997 and 2006:

the number of households increased by 6 million to 24.9 million. The growing trend in people living alone accounted for much of the increase in the number of households and, as a result, the average household size has declined. (McConnell and Wilson, 2007: 2)

Later research in relation to disabled children found that there is often more than one disabled person in a family:

A significant finding of this paper is evidence of a clustering of child and adult disability. First, disabled children were more likely to live with disabled siblings and other disabled children than non-disabled children. One-quarter of children with a DDA defined disability lived with one or more siblings who also had a DDA-defined disability. To date, information on the number of United Kingdom disabled children in any one family unit has been unclear. (Blackburn *et al.*, 2010:11)

While there are fewer people getting married and more couple's co-habiting (McConnell and Wilson, 2007) disabled people however are less likely than non-disabled people to be doing either:

> it has become clear that disabled people are less likely to be married than non-disabled people and more likely to remain single ... Therefore, the large differences in rates of being married appear to be reflecting two distinct patterns: First, a lower propensity to get married among disabled people. Second, a higher propensity for those who do get married will separate and eventually divorce. (Clark and McKay, 2008: 42)

Also the more recent legal recognition of same sex couples and Civil Partnerships has provided a way of recording their relationships, there was an early peak reflecting those who were waiting for the legislation. It is not clear if there are any differences for disabled lesbians or disabled gay men: 'There were a total of 7,169 civil partnerships registered in the United Kingdom in 2008, a fall of 18 per cent on the previous year' (ONS 2010: 22).

According to statistics obtained from Clark and McKay (2008: 37) disabled people are less likely to be in partner relationships than non disabled people:

Having an LLTI [Limiting Long Term Illness] or health problem is associated with:

- a higher proportion of people remaining single; and
- a lower proportion of people being in their first marriage, or being married at all – a slightly lower proportion are cohabiting

The differences in the characteristics of the disabled and non-disabled population account for a large part of the disparity in rates of marriage:

- a higher proportion of disabled people are divorced or separated
- a higher proportion experience bereavement

Cohabiting is commoner among younger adults, and again Clark and McKay (2008: 40) identify a difference for disabled people: 'Controlling for age, disabled people are less likely to cohabit, as well as less likely to be married.'

In Morris's (1989) study of women with spinal injuries 17 out of 102 who were married at the time of their injury had subsequently divorced and while some account for this by individual reactions to their impairment, social expectations also played a role:

> Samantha blames her divorce partly on her consultant who told her husband that '75 per cent of marriages go bang' and to get rid of the double bed. I am sure this stayed with him and did not give our personal life a chance. He left 15 months after I came home.' (Morris, 1989: 83)

In a review of the literature Clark and McKay (2008) found there to be a difference between people who were already married at the time of the onset of impairment and those who had an impairment at the time of marriage, the former being more likely to break up. The interconnectedness of disability with other forms of disadvantage also makes it difficult to draw strong conclusions of cause and effect:

> Plausibly, disability may be an important cause of changes in family status, as well as a result of such changes – particularly the stressful experience of the ending of a long-term relationship. There may also be important 'intervening' variables that account for some of the difference. On average disabled people are poorer than non-disabled people and people living in poverty are generally less likely to be married. So what looks like an effect of disability – or, at least, an association with disability – may be partly or wholly explained by other differences. Such other differences could include lower incomes or being out of the labour market. (Clark and McKay, 2008: 44)

There are many possible causes of relationship break up for disabled people, some of which may be completely unrelated to impairment or disability, however, the strains of dealing with disablism and not receiving appropriate support can put extra strain on a relationship that may have otherwise survived.

In some cases it will be a genuine choice to live alone, but we should raise questions about the barriers that people encounter, which may lead to disabled people being more likely to live alone than non-disabled people.

Family carers

When there is a disabled person in the family, the whole family experiences the impact. In considering the consequences of disability within the family, both the impact of impairments upon individual members and external economic and social pressures on family life need to be taken into account. Families that include a disabled person are more likely to be living in poor housing, poverty and lacking in emotional support social provision generally when compared to families where no one is disabled. The Office of Disability Issues (2010: online) notes that '29 per cent of children in families with at least one disabled member are in poverty, a significantly higher proportion than the 20 per cent of children in families with no disabled member'.

One of the consequences of poverty and inadequate social services support, whether it is as a result of insufficient funding, oppressive policies or poor social work, is that it will cause disabled people of all ages to be dependent on family and friends for personal assistance. When there is a disabled child in the family, mothers are likely to take on the major tasks associated with their child's impairment and disability (Read, 2000). Adequate social services support where disabled people themselves have control over their lives, should be seen as a contribution towards reducing the dependency that could result from the presence of an impairment. It can of course be argued that the lack of such services, rather than impairment, is the cause of dependent relationships.

Many services are collectively provided to ensure the comfort, security and mobility of the non-disabled population, for example, utilities such as water and fuel suppliers or services such as road maintenance or snow clearance. Disabled people also benefit from such services. However, the efficiency with which they are delivered to a level that affords non-disabled people the opportunity to enjoy a satisfying lifestyle is in contrast to the social commitment to services that would allow disabled people to live independently (Finkelstein and Stuart, 1996).

In the 1990s, those who provide personal assistance (or 'care') within family relationships received official recognition and succeeded in having their own needs considered deserving of welfare support through the *Carers (Recognition and Services) Act, 1995*. The early case for this was made by a combination of arguments: that carers save the state money (Nissel and Bonnerjea, 1982); that the task of caring falls disproportionately on women (Equal Opportunities Commission, 1982); and through highlighting the consequences of a lack of support to families which take on the role (J. Oliver, 1982). In the main carers (62 per cent) are found to be supporting people with physical impairments (NHS Information Centre, 2010: 10).

A great deal of stress can arise from being on either side of this dependency relationship, but solutions that do not accord with the aims of independent living for disabled people can be problematic. The recognition of carers is itself part of the problem because it reinforces the helper–helped relationship that lies at the heart of the creation of dependency, by seeing carers' needs as relative to the 'burden' caused by the disabled person. As a result, some feminists seeking to reduce the exploitation of women (Finch, 1984) have advocated respite for carers by providing short- and long-term residential care to disabled people. Such solutions clearly reinforce the exclusion of disabled people from full citizenship.

Others however (Croft, 1986; Morris, 1991), have argued that the interests of disabled people and women carers can be viewed as compatible if a social model analysis is applied to the issues. In this way what is recognised is not so much the burden on one side of the relationship, that is, the carers, but that the aims of independent living are for disabled people to be free of the dependency it creates. Katbamna *et al.* (2000) argue that relationships are complex and that both carers and disabled people experience stigma, love, exhaustion and commitment. The policy solution therefore lies in collective approaches that are based on the inclusion, not the exclusion of disabled people from mainstream social organisation; in other words the removal of disabling barriers. This fits well with a perspective on the changing roles of families and households:

> While there is a trend to smaller, less complex households, the converse is that more and more people will have commitments and networks beyond its confines. The household, having given up its economic and educational roles in the past, is now increasingly sharing its caring responsibilities with both formal and informal sectors. There is an increasing web of contacts and obligations beyond the household, which in most cases is composed of a single nuclear family unit living together. (Ermish and Murphy, 2006: 19)

Professionals and policy makers often use the phrase 'users and carers' in such a way to that suggests an equal status as participants in the design and delivery of social welfare; while laudable this runs the risk of ignoring the potential conflicts of interest between these groups. On the one hand carers are not being offered a favoured status over those they care for, but on the other it may diminish the voice of disabled people and hinder the struggle to achieve social inclusion. For many individuals and families the creation of carers can ignore the reality of how people live:

> Rather than assuming that the presence of a non-disabled family member creates a relationship of carer and cared-for, it is the relationship between partners, parent and child, siblings, etc. which should be recognised. Some relationships can sustain the giving of personal assistance, some cannot. Some people can facilitate independence for their partner, parent or child, some cannot. Some relationships are abusive and exploitative, some are liberating. To categorise people as carers and dependants is to gloss over all of this. (Morris, 1993b: 40)

While the social model perspective of this debate has gained some recognition, its full implications have yet to be appreciated by the carers' lobby. Buckner and Yeandle (2007: 5) note that, 'Some carers have no choice to care because of the paucity of care services and the huge and complex levels of care that they provide', but they argue for the needs of carers rather than establishing the rights of disabled people to be free of these dependency relationships. There is no hint of recognition that this creates and perpetuates dependency whereby disabled people may not get the opportunity to become independent and responsible citizens, and not know how to manage their own lives.

Aldridge and Becker (1996) argued that, unpalatable though it may be, this approach is necessary given the economic and political realities of a residual welfare system. However, what such arguments do is to reinforce the injustice of the individual model of disability with its acceptance that disability is a welfare, not a civil rights, issue. This may not become obvious to many until parents can no longer do the 'caring' and the impact on all concerned can be negative. Solutions to this dichotomy have rarely been addressed, however one small project used the social model and brought together family carers and disabled people to develop a protocol to work together on areas of agreement, and to manage areas of disagreement at both an individual level and at an organisational level (Thomas and Clark, 2010a).

Some of these issues are beyond the ability of individual social workers to resolve, but their contribution to the administration of welfare can have a determining impact on individuals and families. The message for social workers in relation to the issue of carers is

– do not to make assumptions, but work with people from their own perception of the reality of their lives. In many relationships where at least one partner is disabled no help may be needed at all, for example:

> My wife goes about her daily chores. I earn the living; we have friends who accept us; our bungalow is indistinguishable from the neighbouring bungalows except that possibly ours is a little better kept. My wife helps me to dress; I help her to bath; we have sexual intercourse frequently; we row about my driving; she never has enough housekeeping money; she always lacks something to wear for the special occasion; in fact, it's all very normal. (Shearer, 1981b: 29–30)

With the observation that the gender roles may not be quite so marked in some marriages today, this seems to be a rather ordinary marriage. Working within families is a privilege which requires sensitivity and open mindedness rather than professional judgement based upon politically normative views of complex relationships. Social work intervention needs to include awareness of the range of role expectations on individuals, to avoid stereotyping people and to be conscious of the impact of disability from the perspective of the way people see themselves. Intervention should not proceed on the assumption that impairments may create relationship problems; even where such problems are present, they may stem from outside rather than from individual impairments and hence form another aspect of the process of disability.

Relationships

Culture, community, social life and diversity

Relationships can range from acquaintances through friends, family and close personal and sexual partners. Many disabled people have fulfilling relationships much the same as anyone else. However, for some there are specific issues which arise due to limitations from impairment and/or limitations imposed by societal systems and cultural pressures. These issues could lead to difficulties in establishing and maintaining relationships. Disabled people are present in all communities, including Black and Minority Ethnic communities, and their cultural expectations vary enormously. Many follow the expectations of the dominant culture of the United Kingdom, while others maintain the expectations of their cultural origins. Within United Kingdom dominant cultures there are sub cultures including regional differences and differences related to socio-economic class. In some communities and faith groups there is an expectation that family members will marry within their own networks, sometimes the marriages are arranged by mutual agreement, (occasionally they may be forced where either or both the bride and groom do not want to marry). Where families arrange marriages spouses are also sought for disabled family members in a similar way to non-disabled family members.

Most disabled people are heterosexual, as is the case in the rest of the population. Likewise many disabled people are lesbians and gay men, and they face additional issues compared to either straight disabled people or gay non-disabled people. This is more complicated than simply adding two types of experience together. Within the disabled people's community disabled lesbians and gay men may encounter homophobia, while in the gay community they may encounter disablism. Research by Avante Consultancy (2006: 16) found that:

> Whilst respondents did confirm that they had encountered the physical access barriers that affect many people with a disability, regardless of their sexual orientation, the most significant barriers were a lack of awareness, prejudice, and ignorance about LGBT [lesbian, gay, bisexual and transgender] and/or disability issues and, frequently, homophobia.

There are specific issues for young disabled people who have experienced only segregation and 'special' education. People who acquire an impairment in later life may find that their relationships change and their networks are not so easy to maintain. There are expectations as people age that the types of relationships they have will change, particularly in relation to sexual relationships which may be considered to be less important as people grow older.

Disabled people and non-disabled people inhabit rather different worlds, for example the location of many social gatherings, such as house parties, bars, clubs, are often physically inaccessible. Disabled people may find it difficult to initiate contacts in pubs or at parties, and taking a seat close to someone is often difficult for wheelchair users or for visually impaired people. Wheelchair users who approach a group of people who are standing chatting are likely to find there is an expectation that they are trying to pass through rather than join in, and even if they get into the circle the conversation is physically above their heads. Young people with mobility impairments may find it is not always possible to participate in that favourite teenage pastime of hanging around on street corners. Parents of disabled young people may have been overprotective and reluctant to allow their children to take the usual teenage risks. An important part of growing up and growing away from parents is to take risks and do things that parents would probably not approve of; disabled teenagers who rely on their parents for transport can't lie to their parents about where they have been or who they have been with.

Attitudes and reactions of others

Another major problem for disabled people in making and sustaining relationships is the reaction of other people. Some people may be prejudiced against disabled people as individuals or as a group, or indeed they may simply be uncertain about how to treat him or her – should the person's impairment be ignored, or spoken about openly, and, if the latter, at what stage in the relationship should such questions be raised? Lenny and Sercombe (2002: 17) suggest that avoiding communication with disabled people

> is often interpreted as hostility, either because of the way that people with able bodies look at those with disabilities or because of their avoidance of interaction, may more frequently be due to uncertainty about how to interact, about reluctance to draw undue attention to themselves or the person with a disability or to invade their privacy.

When people have contact with each other as equals, particularly when they are working toward common aims, prejudice disappears or does not occur in the first place. However, the separate development that comes about through segregation in education, employment, transport and so on, as well as negative media images can only contribute to the lack of positive contact. For young disabled people a major factor is the experience of overprotection, by parents and special schools that fail to equip them with the ability to develop relationships. They may be unsure or lack experience about how to present themselves to other people, this has often been put down to lack of opportunity or lack of emotional and social skills (Stewart, 1979), which may be so but there is more to it than that. One issue is the reactions and attitudes of non-disabled people, who have themselves had an education away from disabled children, and are unlikely to know how to relate to disabled people. If an impairment is acquired later in life some people may also internalise societal and cultural expectations and simply accept that they are no longer a part of the world they formerly inhabited.

Sexuality and sexual relationships

The expression of sexuality and having sexual relationships can contribute to well-being, however the attention paid to sex and disabled people has tended to focus on problems (Stewart, 1979; Felce and Perry, 1997; Tepper, 1999). This has led to the manner in which subsequent interventions have occurred as being 'unhelpful because they are mechanistic, depoliticised, and outdated' (Shakespeare, 1997: 183). In fact, it could be argued that this aspect of disabled people's lives has received too much attention and that it should be returned to where it belongs – to people's private lives. Certainly it is true to say that the attention attracted by the 'sex and disability industry' reveals as much about society's own values as it does about the sexual aspects of the lives of disabled people.

Assumptions made by some professionals that sexual relations are an inevitable problem for disabled people and their partners are unwarranted. Disabled people are sexual beings with desires and participate in sexual relationships much the same way as non-disabled people. However Western popular culture puts pressure on many people to conform to certain expectations of sexuality, they are conveyed in commercial advertising and popular maga-zines and websites giving advice on how to attract a mate.

There is little empirical evidence about whether the proportion of disabled people experiencing sexual difficulties is greater than the rest of the population or not, though Morris (1989) adds a more qualitative dimension to the meaning of that experience for women with spinal injuries, while Shakespeare *et al.* (1996) have contributed significantly to the literature with their biographical and analytical account of sexuality focussing on gay and lesbian relationships. The relevance of this discussion for social work intervention is that it would be wrong to assume that all disabled people have unresolved sexual problems of one kind or another, but that when it is apparent that there are sexual problems it might be useful to have some understanding of possible causes. Pain or lack of sensation may be factors which make it difficult to achieve satisfactory sexual fulfilment for both parties, as can impotence, depending upon the particular medical condition. Real or imagined physical danger can also affect sexual enjoyment, as can the side-effects of some medication. Incontinence and incontinence devices may also inhibit or affect sexual relations. Finally, it has been clearly established that psychological factors like fear, anxiety and a poor self-image can also adversely affect sexual performance.

Many people, whether they are disabled or not, do not achieve the cultural and media portrayals of sexual performance. The problem then may be one of social expectations and cultural values rather than impaired individual performance, though of course the discrepancy between social expectations and individual performance may be experienced as personal inadequacy. Shakespeare (1996: 192) explains how these expectations operate:

> In the realm of sex and love, the generalised assumption that disability is a medical tragedy becomes dominant and inescapable. In modern western societies, sexual agency is considered the essential element of full adult personhood, replacing the role formerly taken by paid work: because disabled people are infantilised, and denied the status of active subjects, consequently their sexuality is undermined. This also works the other way, in that the assumption of asexuality is a contributing factor towards the disregard of disabled people.

The social model of disability may also throw light on the sexual problems of disabled people in day-centres and residential establishments; problems are often created by segregating disabled people in particular kinds of institution, and the (often informal) rules made in them to regulate all behaviour, which often extends to disabled people's own homes when they are receiving community care services. There may well be moral dilemmas about issues like helping disabled people to masturbate if they are unable to do it themselves, or putting them in a bed of their choice and not where members of staff think they should be. However, problems created by non-disabled people organising services in particular ways are often turned around and located at the level of individual disabled people. The practice of social work within a social model would require an end to this process of pathologising and the development of an awareness of the support that individuals might need when faced with such barriers.

Parenting

Throughout the twentieth century there were attempts in many western countries, ranging from segregation to sterilisation, to prevent disabled people, especially those with learning difficulties, from having children and this eugenicist impulse is still present in the concerns of many in the welfare field. While there are preconceptions of asexuality, many disabled people are parents. It is useful to note that 'about 12 per cent (1.7 million) of Britain's 14.1 million parents are disabled and 1.1 million households with dependent children have at least one disabled parent' (Morris and Wates, 2006: 15).

According to the *Families and Children Study*, the types of impairment that disabled mothers have include 'problems with arms, legs, hands, feet, neck or back including arthritis or rheumatism (47 per cent); depression or other mental illness (26 per cent); and chest or breathing-related problems such as asthma and bronchitis (17 per cent)' (Morris and Wates, 2006: 16).

However, an earlier more in-depth study by Goodinge (2000) found there were somewhere between 1.2 and 4 million disabled parents in the United Kingdom, more than two-thirds of them women, this number is growing. In her inspection of eight social service authorities she identified 621 disabled parents receiving services, the majority of whom (61 per cent) had physical impairments while 12 per cent had learning difficulties. However, about one-fifth of all these families were treated as child protection cases and this rose to about two-thirds when the parents had learning difficulties. Both these figures are high and seem to suggest that social workers are not that likely to provide support for disabled parents without an element of concern for the protection of the child. None of the authorities Goodinge inspected had any system for identifying families with disabled parents and as such offering support was not routine.

Wates (2004: 137) argued that the dominant cultural attitudes in which disabled people are depicted as vulnerable, incapable and dependent lead to childcare policies in which 'the (mainly non-disabled) children of disabled parents come to be seen as the primary "clients" and the potential recipients of services, rather than the disabled adults with parenting responsibility for those children'.

She also points out that when disabled parents have been involved with social services, the provision of services improved

(Wates, 2002). Meanwhile advice to disabled people from the United Kingdom's government's website at the end of 2010 is promising: 'It's important to remember that your assessment as a disabled person/parent is about your needs. If you receive the right support, your child's needs will be met without the need for services from the "Children and families team"' (Direct Gov, 2010: online).

Local authorities are reminded in *Putting People First* (Department of Health, 2010a: 11) that 'In the course of assessing an individual's needs, councils should recognise that adults who have parenting responsibilities for a child under 18 years may require help with these responsibilities'.

Whether this transpires into the right support at the right time is debateable when it seems that the children of disabled parents are treated as young carers. This assumption of dependency can have profound effects on families and in particular where caring by a child for a parent becomes a form of role reversal. Keith and Morris (1995) argue that this has the effect of denying the ability of disabled people to parent. Research in this area has tended to assume that the presence of an impairment is the cause of the need to care rather than inadequate community support services. The demand for more support based on carers' needs both ignores the reality of the situation and attributes blame to disabled people. Rather than focussing on young carers as an inevitable role, social workers using the social model will consider how to ensure disabled parents have the support they need to be parents.

While some disabled people will need support to be able to parent a child, services are often geared towards a concept of dangerousness and issues of disability are inappropriately conflated with issues of drug misuse and domestic violence:

> Children grow up with adults, who have a major impact on their development and well-being, and some of the risk factors for children flow from parents' physical and learning disabilities, mental health and substance misuse problems, and the incidence of domestic violence. The risks to be managed, and issues associated with safeguarding and personal liberty, in Adult Services are equivalent to those in Children's Services. (ADASS, 2009: 4)

This view makes the case for the continuing involvement of professionals rather than looking at ways that disabled parents could be supported to parent their children. A clear example of this is the criteria by which a disabled parent would become eligible for the care component of Disability Living Allowance (DLA). Rather than being asked what they need in order to carry out their parental responsibilities they have to demonstrate that they are a risk to their child without the supervision of another person. Goodinge (2000: 2) comments on the inappropriateness of social services being provided outside a social model:

> We were concerned to find that although, according to senior managers, the social model of disability guided the council's work this did not follow through into their staff's actions. The focus of staff appeared to be either on the children in the family or on the impact of the adults' disability on their personal needs. Workers rarely looked beyond this and seldom focused on the whole family and how to support and help the parents in the discharge of their parental duties in their social setting.

Goodinge (2000: 2) made recommendations on the principles underpinning the services provided recommending:

> A philosophical and practical shift in the approach to working with disabled parents is required. It needs to be underpinned by:
>
> • a recognition of the right of disabled people, within the bounds of current legislation, to be supported in fulfilling their roles and responsibilities as parents.

Although her report concentrates on the ways in which practice might be administratively enforced, it is worth noting the extent to which the social model of disability is accepted by those in authority and their expectations that this should be the guiding principle for social work interventions.

Priestley (2003) argues that disabled people have not just been considered as incapable of parenting, but are often subjected to surveillance rather than support. He points to a number of user-led initiatives which do offer support in non-intrusive ways. These include advocacy and direct payments which will be discussed in more depth in Chapter 4. The challenge for social workers is to respect disabled people's rights while providing sufficient support that will enable disabled parents to take full responsibility for child rearing, without the necessity for surveillance based solely on the presence of impairment.

Disabled children

The birth of a disabled child can be a traumatic and shattering event for a family and that is the dominant way both professionals and researchers have treated the subject. As a consequence it has usually been assumed that as well as needing appropriate information and practical assistance parents also need skilled help to overcome the loss, grief and bereavement they feel as a consequence of failing to produce a healthy child (Selfe and Stow, 1981). However, this view does not pass completely unchallenged, and others have suggested that the birth of a disabled child does not, of necessity, promote adverse emotional reactions (Roith, 1974; Avery, 1997).

Where stress is present, it may stem from unresolved practical problems and the link between disability and poverty:

> There is a two-way relationship between disability and poverty in childhood. Disabled children are among the most likely to experience poverty and poor children are more likely to be become disabled than those who are better off. In 2002/2003, 29 per cent of people with one or more disabled children in the household lived in poverty, compared with 21 per cent of households with no disabled children. It is well established that persistent poverty during childhood has significant scarring effects on life chances but it also impacts on childhood experiences. (IPPR, 2007: 6)

Thus, in discussing how having a disabled child impacts upon family life, differing views based upon the individual and social models of disability again emerge. In recognition of the many frustrations encountered by families with disabled children there was a social policy response in 2007 in the form of *Aiming High for Disabled Children*, bringing with it dedicated resources and a Disabled Children's Standard with themes which promote independence, early intervention and multi-agency planning (Department for Education, 2007). However more recent research indicates that this has not had the intended impact with disabled children still being disadvantaged:

> Disabled children lived in different personal situations from their non-disabled counterparts, and were more likely to live with low-income, deprivation, debt and poor housing. This was particularly the case for disabled children from black/minority ethnic/mixed parentage groups and lone-parent households. Childhood disability was associated with lone parenthood and

parental disability and these associations persisted when social disadvantage was controlled for. (Blackburn *et al.*, 2010:1)

The lack of practical help has huge impacts on family relationships; where there is a disabled child with significant support needs parents may find that they do not receive enough help and relationships can suffer:

> More than half of families who responded to our survey (55 per cent) said that the opportunity to spend time with their spouse or partner away from the role of caring is poor. Some children with disabilities require a significant amount of care and treatment day and night. As one parent is often unable to work, the other parent may work long hours to boost the family income. Many of the comments show that the demands of caring leaves very little time for each other and couples sometimes lead separate social lives because whilst one is caring, the other is snatching a couple of hours rest or time with other children. In some cases the parents have no social life at all. Research has shown parents with disabled children are more likely to experience a relationship breakdown than parents of non-disabled children. (Bennett, 2009:13)

Families in this study were asked to list the top three things from a multiple choice question about what would make them stronger socially, the answers showed the priorities of families which included:

- leisure time for the whole family (46 per cent)
- specific play activities for disabled children (42 per cent)
- community/society needs better understanding (37 per cent)
- to have unbroken nights (30 per cent)
- meeting other families in similar situations (7 per cent)
- to have a local children's centre (5 per cent). (Adapted from Bennett, 2009: 23)

Social workers often seek solutions through offering direct service provision, so it is interesting that children's centres are so low down on the list. Families using direct payments may not think in terms of services at all and so use the money in creative ways. Bennett (2009: 23) comments on families' requirement for practical support:

> Many of the respondents' comments give an insight into the difficulty of accessing practical help, which would enable families to

lead the lives they want to lead. Most families talk of the stress and frustration that comes from having to fight for the smallest amount of support and it is apparent that those families less able to battle the system are particularly vulnerable.

Certainly it can be part of the social worker's job to help in the organising and adapting that is required, this can include making sure the family is receiving all the financial benefits it is entitled to, contacting organisations like the *Family Fund* where necessary, and negotiating with other agencies such as housing departments. It is also necessary however, for social workers to assess and provide a range of services and direct payments from their own agencies, particularly if they are working in the statutory sector. Issues about practical support will be returned to in Chapter 4.

Growing up

Growing up and leaving school, can be challenging for any young person, but disabled young people often face additional problems of low expectations, a lack of continuous service provision, unmet needs in further and higher education, and a disproportionate like-lihood of not being in education, employment or training (IPPR, 2007). Parents who have had to fight for services can find it partic-ularly hard to 'let go' of their son and daughter and allow them to find their own way in the world.

Whereas this is generally known to be part of growing up for disabled children and young people, the involvement with organi-sations means this period of life becomes a transition between serv-ices. At an organisational level the lack of communication between services, which provide support for disabled children and young people, and services for disabled adults has been identified as a problem. The *Disabled Persons (Services, Consultation and Representation) Act 1986* specifically addressed this issue in sections 5 and 6 which laid down a framework for these two agen-cies to communicate with each other in order to ensure the trans-fer of responsibility and a smooth transition for disabled adolescents to adult services. However this issue requires more than administrative procedures, there is the need for interrelated policy making between children's and adult services. Also young disabled people should be included in the policy-making process, the development of social work skills in working with families with disabled children, and for the use of disability equality training as a means of promoting the social model of disability. Despite the rhetoric of joined-up services since 1997, there has been little change in practice. Furthermore, there is a need to go beyond the two agencies that are by statute required to communicate and to involve GPs, health authorities, housing departments and employers in the process. Each of these contribute to the production of a disabling environments and therefore need to make changes to their own practices if disabled children are to be enabled to enter adult life with the opportunities available to non-disabled people.

Growing old with impairment and disability

It is not the intention to deal separately with the topic of social work with older people, for this has been covered by a number of other writers (for example, Phillips *et al.*, 2006; Crawford and Walker, 2008) in relation to the responsibilities of social services towards older people when they acquire impairments. It is the ageing of people who have had impairment from a younger age that needs to be considered here, although much of it will be relevant to the former group.

In the past, few people with impairments would have survived into old age and so virtually nothing was known about what happens to disabled people as they grow old. However, in the late twentieth century disabled people were living longer and some researchers (Morris, 1989; Zarb *et al.*, 1990; Zarb, 1991; 1993) began to examine the issues and consequences for the provision of supportive environments. Zarb (1993) argued that it is important to have a conceptual framework for understanding this issue as traditional psychological concepts of ageing and policy analyses tend to be inadequate to explain the personal, physical and social consequences of ageing with an impairment and disability.

While each individual will experience ageing differently, there are certain commonalities in terms of both individual problems associated with impairment and social problems that result from the way society responds to disabled people as they age. Zarb (1993: 190) describes some of the individual issues:

> many of the physical changes that people experience are perceived as being long-term effects of their original impairments. For some groups, there are also common secondary impairments caused either by the original impairment, or the long term effects of medical treatment or rehabilitation.

Individual impairments may be exacerbated as a result of ageing and as a consequence the need for personal assistance will increase. However, current social policy tends to assume the opposite because it reflects the role expectations of society which are artificially linked to chronological age, this involvement with systems and organisations involves another transition. In this way the spending limits of social service authorities on adult social care which are set relative to residential and nursing home payments, are considerably lower for people over retirement age than for those of working age, while direct payments may be discouraged if the person is aged over 65. Similarly, welfare benefit payments are usually reduced at retirement age and some, such as the financial support for mobility disappear altogether, causing a real drop in income to people who may have had very restricted opportunities to earn personal pensions in the same way as the non-disabled population.

Becoming older often causes people to reflect more on their earlier lives and for some disabled people such reflections may amount to a reminiscence of unfulfilled potentials. MacFarlane (1994) argued that for disabled women in particular this may be a time when they recall a lifetime of being deprived of the right to enjoy fulfilling relationships, of being aware of one's own sexuality and of experiencing childbirth, and that this can prove to be a daunting task. Furthermore, while this is itself a result of the social responses to impairment over a lifetime, it can be compounded by the policy and institutional systems whereby older people's services do not provide the same level of support for younger adults: 'It is agonising to look forward to the struggle of reaching the age of sixty and to know that hard fought for services and other provision will be reassessed and probably changed because of the ageing process' (MacFarlane, 1994: 255).

Ageing therefore may be experienced as a time of threat, not simply from the difficulties caused by deteriorating health or emotional distress, but by the systems of welfare agencies, in particular their readiness to view residential care as a more appropriate response to the need for personal assistance. Zarb (1993) suggests that this threat to lifestyle may be so great as to cause some people to consider euthanasia or suicide – a terrible indictment of the role that social services play in providing 'care' to disabled people as they grow older. Clearly then, the task for social workers as agents of such authorities must be to assist individuals to access the services that will permit them to maintain independence and choice within their own lives. Once again it is necessary to have an awareness of the

individual problems that disabled people face, but it is more important to understand how these become barriers when policy
responses follow an individual model of disability.

CHAPTER OVERVIEW
- Social workers need to keep an open mind about whether
  problems present or not.
- Problems could be:
  o individual problems of a personal or sexual nature,
  o problems related to lack of resources or practical
    provisions, and
  o discrepancies between individual behaviour and social
    expectations.
- Social workers should take account of the possible
  presence of some of these factors and should encourage
  disabled people to take their place in the world and not
  be segregated from it in schools, day centres and
  residential units.
- Solutions to problems may be found by working with
  individuals and their families to identify disabling barriers
  beyond impairment.
- Disabled adults, disabled children and their families deal
  with the same issues as the rest of the population across
  the whole life course and including those in Black and
  Minority Ethnic (BME) and faith communities, and in the
  lesbian and gay communities.
- However disabled people face additional issues
  emanating from societal systems and cultural expectations
  and pressures.
- Social workers need to be alert to the many societal and
  cultural influences which are imposed on top of the effects
  of impairment.

Points for reflection

Exercise 1

Most of us are able to exercise a great deal of autonomy in deciding
what we need to enhance our own lives. Consider why the state has
decided it is necessary to have trained professionals to decide this
for disabled people. Try to answer the following questions:

- Why is it necessary for a social worker to assess the needs of a disabled person?
- What problems would arise if disabled people assessed their own needs?
- Now apply your answers to yourself and consider what difference it would make to your life if someone else was making these decisions for you.

Exercise 2

- Make a list of three medical conditions with which you are familiar. Make nine further lists of the range of social needs that might arise for people from three different socio-economic backgrounds with each of these conditions.
- Examine the lists and think about whether the needs which arise are more likely to be linked directly to the medical condition or to the socio-economic backgrounds

Further resources

Morris, J. (1993) *Independent Lives: Community Care and Disabled People* (Basingstoke, Macmillan).

Shakespeare, T., Gillespie-Sells, K. and Davies, D. (1996) *The Sexual Politics of Disability: Untold Desires* (London, Cassell).
A valuable contribution to literature on disabled people and sexuality focussing on gay and lesbian relationships.

Thomas, P. and Clark, L. (2010a) Building Positive Partnerships: An agreement between Family Carer's Organisations, Disabled People's Organisations, Deaf People's Organisations and User Led Organisations (Manchester: Breakthrough UK).
A protocol which was produced by disabled people and carers organisations working together on how to work together.

Zarb, G. (1993) 'The dual experience of ageing with a disability', in J. Swain, V. Finkelstein, S. French and M. Oliver (eds.) *Disabling Barriers – Enabling Environments*, London, Sage.
This chapter explores changes in the experience of impairment and dealing with transition to older people's services and systems.

Breakthrough UK is a disabled people's organisation which conducts social model research and consultancy (among other things): www.breakthrough-uk.co.uk/

Carers UK provides a support network for carers: http://www.carersuk.org/

Disabled Parents Network is a support network for disabled parents, led by disabled parents: www.disabledparentsnetwork.org.uk/

Shaping Our Lives is an independent user-controlled organisation, think tank and network with a vision of a society which is equal and fair where all people have the same opportunities, choices, rights and responsibilities: www.shapingourlives.org.uk/index.html

CHAPTER 4

Independent living and personal assistance

Introduction

During the 1970s disabled people became increasingly dissatisfied with the lack of choice and control in their lives, inevitably this involved dissatisfaction with the professionals who offer support. Over the decades disabled people have campaigned for and achieved an increase in their choice and control over personal assistance and receiving direct payments has made a major contribution to this. The campaigns and eventual support systems for those in receipt of direct payments has come through disabled people's own organisations in the form of Centres for Independent Living (CILs) these organisations also offers support in other areas of Independent Living.

Centres for Independent Living

The moves toward independent living did not come from professionals, policy makers or family carers, but from disabled people themselves in the 1970s. This can be traced back to the US where Centres for Independent Living (CILs) began. At Berkeley University, with the help of a small Federal grant Ed Roberts and other students started the Physically Disabled Students Program. In 1972 they set up the first Centre for Independent Living (CIL), which was independent of the university, so that disabled people could support each other in finding jobs, housing and personal support. In the US the CILs were successful in gaining Federal and State funds in order to take over the provision of services for disabled people. The CILs were able to reject the institutional solutions that had been provided in the past in favour of disabled people being in control of the way services were provided (Shearer, 1984). Eventually their campaigning went beyond restructuring of welfare with the passing of comprehensive anti-discrimination legislation in the United States with the *Disabilities Act 1990* (Oliver, 1996). However, 80 per cent of the

Medicaid budget for support to disabled people was still spent on nursing homes into the twenty-first century.

These campaigns were taken up in the United Kingdom when disabled people set up the first CILs in the early 1980s in Hampshire and later Southampton. In 1984 one of the most successful CILs was set up in Derbyshire; its founders adopted the term 'integrated living' rather than 'independent living' (Davis, 1984). These CILs were established using the social model of disability. The Derbyshire Coalition of Disabled People identified seven elements of primary needs for disabled people to be independent. These became known as the seven needs of independent living and are still used as the basis of CILs; they came about following a great deal of discussion between disabled people about what was needed to be integrated into the community:

> No move was possible without first thinking of housing; it was *housing* design which facilitated the efficient use of certain *technical aids*; and those two elements in combination had a dramatic effect on the amount of *personal assistance* needed to make the whole scheme work.
>
> What also became clear was the fact that simply having *access to information* was not in itself enough ... There was an element of *advice and counselling* involved in translating and turning information into practical use ... *accessible transport* – some way of making journeys outside the home – and then that of *environmental access*. The benefit of having accessible transport could not be fully experienced, if disabled people were confronted with insurmountable physical, barriers when they reached the destination of their choice.

From the point of view of disabled people who were setting out to achieve full social integration from the extremity of social deprivation in segregated residential institutions, these seven elements were encountered in the following logical order (Davis, 1990: 6–7; emphasis added):

- information
- counselling
- housing
- technical aids
- personal assistance
- transport
- access

Hampshire CIL and Southampton CIL added another five needs (which Davis would have described as 'secondary' needs) to arrive at the '12 basic rights' which are needed to achieve independent living:

- inclusive Education and Training
- an adequate Income
- equal opportunities for Employment
- advocacy (towards self-advocacy)
- appropriate and Accessible Heath Care Provision
(Southampton CIL, 2010: online)

Organisations *of* disabled people achieved a notable success in campaigning for and demonstrating the advantages of direct payments, and for the involvement of service users in supporting people using direct payments.

In the late 1990s the British Council of Organisations of Disabled People set up the National Centre for Independent Living (NCIL) which took a lead role in the campaign for disabled people to receive direct payments in order to manage their own personal assistants (Evans, 2002). NCIL was able to support some local organisations to run Personal Assistant Schemes, such as that operated by the Greenwich Association of Disabled People (GAD) which employed a Personal Assistance Advisor to help individuals with the problems they might encounter by becoming an employer. An evaluation of this scheme after three years of its operating concluded that:

developing independent living options like Personal Assistance Schemes is not just morally desirable and professionally appropriate, but also offers the possibility of providing more cost effective and efficient services through switching from the over-production of services that people don't want or need and the underproduction of those that they do, to a situation where the services that are produced and purchased by statutory providers are precisely the services that users want and need. (Oliver and Zarb, 1992: 13)

While CILs may be few in numbers in the United Kingdom, their impact on the lives of those who have used their services contrasts markedly with their experience of social work (Barnes *et al.*, 2001).

The work of those involved in the campaigns for user control had an impact on social policy as evidenced in the *Improving the Life Chances of Disabled People* report which described Centres for Independent Living as:

grassroots organisations run and controlled by disabled people. Their aims are to assist disabled people take control over their lives and achieve full participation in society ... For most CILs their main activity, and source of income, is running support schemes to enable disabled people to use Direct Payments. Such schemes may involve: advice and information; advocacy and peer support; assistance with recruiting and employing Personal Assistants (PAs); a payroll service; a register of PAs; and training of PAs. (Prime Minister's Strategy Unit, 2005: 84)

The *Life Chances* report also recommended that each Local Authority area should support the setting up of a User Led Organisation based on CILs and this was reaffirmed in the *Putting People First* protocol document (Department of Health, 2007: 4). Funding was made available via the Department of Health for a programme to assist local authorities in supporting the development of a user-led organisation in their area.

CILs have enabled disabled people to be in control of how their support is provided. Unlike the institutionalised approach of social services departments, which often result in moral judgements about what disabled people may or may not expect from the welfare system, CILs are notable developments because they listen and respect the service user as a citizen, with all that entails. They offer support in arranging practical assistance which may in many cases be paramount. The role for social workers may be crucial in assisting with locating and providing appropriate resources which should include making best use of the services offered by the local CIL. This once again suggests a shift in focus, away from the individual model and towards a social model of disability; keeping the 12 basic rights of independent living in mind will assist in this shift.

Personal assistants and direct payments

A key role for CILs in the United Kingdom has been that of running schemes which provide practical advice and support to disabled people in employing and managing their own personal assistants. This is vital in supporting more choice and control over everyday support. In order to employ personal assistants disabled people need direct payments. The *National Assistance Act*, 1948 placed the responsibility and funds for providing personal care services with local authorities and while they were permitted to directly supply or purchase care from private or voluntary organisations, it was illegal for them to make payments to individuals for personal care. This prevented groups of disabled people from developing in the way that CILs had in the United States.

An opportunity for disabled people in the United Kingdom to receive cash to manage their own support came in 1988 with the setting up of the Independent Living Fund (ILF), which provided cash to top up services received from Local Authorities. It gave large numbers of disabled people with high support needs access to funds for this purpose, and from their point of view it is a tremendous success, demand far outstripped the government's expectations. In 1993 more responsibility was absorbed by local authorities following implementation of the NHS and Community Care Act, 1990. There were 22,000 people in receipt of payments from the Independent Living Fund when it closed in 1992 (Morris, 1993a: 171) these people were transferred to the ILF extension fund. Another ILF fund was set up for new applicants who would require additional financial contribution from local authorities.

Those in receipt of ILF monies, and other disabled people who relied purely on Local Authority services, still criticised direct service provision as being too rigid and hindering independence and inclusion. Their calls for more autonomy resulted in a policy agreement that disabled people could arrange their own support. The Community Care (Direct Payments) Act, 1996 made it legal for local authorities to support individual personal assistance schemes with cash payments to disabled people rather than providing them with services. Initially the scheme was not mandatory, but in April 2004 the Secretary of State for Health required local authorities to provide direct payments under powers given to him in the Health and Social Care Act, 2001. Direct payments helped to overcome many of the problems experienced in relation to the provision of adequate support services. However, the transfer of employer responsibilities from local authorities to individual disabled people also requires disabled people to have the skills in the recruitment, management and administration of the service and this is where the expertise of CILs is required.

Alongside the development of direct payments the ILF continued and by 2006 there were 18,000 people using it. However in 2010 it was announced that ILF will stop taking new applicants, they are now expected to obtain all their support from Local Authorities.

Direct payments have the potential to radically change the relationship between disabled people and those who provide their 'care'. Yet some local authorities have been slow to ensure that disabled people have access to the kind of support a CIL can offer. Barnes *et al.* (2004: 10) found:

> a general pattern whereby many traditional Labour controlled local authorities have failed to develop direct payments. Conversely, in Conservative administrations – particularly where there is a strong user-led support organisation – recipients have increased significantly.

Also in their most recent inspection report the CSCI (2009: x–xi) identified certain barriers to disabled people receiving direct payments which includes difficulties in shifting the emphasis from people's impairments to disabling barriers and 'mixed views held by local councillors, staff and people using services and their families about the concept, feasibility and application of personal budgets'.

Davey *et al.* (2007) in their survey found that local authorities had reservations that contributed to their not implementing direct payments. This included service users and carers concerns about managing the payments, staff resistance and a difficulty in finding personal assistants. Having an effective support scheme was high on the list of factors that assist in setting up direct payments schemes.

Given all the hurdles it seems to be quite an achievement for any disabled person to gain direct payments:

> If a local authority engages only reluctantly with direct payments, fails to support its staff, designs very bureaucratic and unresponsive systems, and fails to support to provide appropriate advice and support, then we should hardly be surprised if only the most determined and confident people fight their way through the system to get access. (Glasby and Littlechild, 2009: 42)

However central government (even with the change of political control) has remained committed to direct payments and disabled people certainly want them. Direct payments have been extended to all people who are eligible for community care services. Local authorities have the power (but not a duty) to offer direct payments to people who lack mental capacity where there is responsible person to manage the payment.

In the financial year 2009/10, 166,000 adults aged 18 and over received direct payments. This is an increase of 24 per cent from 86,000 in 2008/09 (NHS Information centre, 2011a: 41). And there is a corresponding rise in expenditure on direct payments:

There has been a sharp rise in the amount of money spent by councils on Direct Payments, with an increase of 31 per cent between 2008–09 and 2009–10 in real terms. The amount spent on Direct Payments equates to 5 per cent (£815 million) of the overall gross current expenditure for adults in 2009–10. (NHS Information Centre, 2011b: 11)

However this is still a small proportion of expenditure.

Another significant development in independent living is that of personal budgets whereby all disabled people who are assessed as requiring a service are advised how much money is being allowed for their support package, this may be taken in part or in its entirety as a direct payment. The idea for personal budgets came from work with people with learning difficulties and the *Valuing People* programme. They have been promoted by family carers of people with learning difficulties, especially through organisations such as *In Control*. The aim is to have direction and control over the type of support required, while the management of the budget remains with the Local Authority. Although the origins are quite different from that of direct payments, personal budgets are welcomed by disabled people.

In addition another initiative of the Welfare Reform Act 2009 is the *Right to Control* scheme which gives disabled adults a legal right to exercise choice and control over support they receive from places other than social services. These consist of assistance from employment support programmes *Access to Work* and *Work Choice* and non-statutory housing support *Supporting People*. The scheme will also cover other services which are covered by different legislation, the *Independent Living Fund*, *Disabled Facilities Grants* and *Adult Social Care*. The idea is that people will have individual budgets and the option of direct payments to cover their entitlement to these programmes (Department of Health, 2010c).

In addition there have been pilots of personal health budgets for individuals to have more control over designing and managing their own support (Department of Health, 2010c).

This co-production where people using services are involved in their design and management requires professionals to hand over control. Hunter and Ritchie (2007: 155) support the idea, but point out:

> Co-production isn't a magical solution to the seemingly intractable problem of why services set out with good intentions but end up too often with poor results. It does, however, invite professionals to reconsider the 'We'll fix it' response to people requiring services and to become intolerant of systemic incompetence. A shared recognition of the limitations of the human services system is the first step in co-creating more sustaining and sustainable communities.

Hunter and Ritchie (2007) also point out that co-production is a philosophy not a model.

If social workers are committed to the delivery of non-stigmatised services, then direct payments probably offers them their best opportunity since 1948 to do so. Just as senior managers and councillors found it difficult to delegate the responsibility for budgets to caseworkers as was envisaged in *Caring for People* (Department of Health, 1989), social workers have been resisting handing over such responsibility to disabled people (Sapey and Pearson, 2002). Social workers should work with disabled people to put the case for this change within their agencies. Once in place social workers and care managers need to relinquish part of their responsibility for the purchasing or provision of community care services and to support individuals in running their own personal assistance schemes. Their role is to ensure that the administration of these monies, the ways in which disabled people are required to account for their use, is managed in a manner that is helpful to the aims of independent living, and not in ways that replicate the barriers of institutionalised care.

Assessment

Although more disabled people have new options for choice and control there is a long standing legal requirement for an assessment of their needs. Bell and Klemz (1981: 117) note that:

> In social services departments, the purpose of assessing the needs of physically handicapped clients is to bring to them the appropriate services which councils provide and to advise on other services that may be required.

Doyal and Gough (1991) describe the professional assessment of need as a 'colonialist' approach in that it involves one group determining what is best for another less powerful group of people. They argued for an objective and universal approach to the notion of need and suggest that one of the principal benefits of this is to clearly separate the arguments over what needs exist from the issue of how and to what extent society may be willing to meet those needs. The move from assessing eligibility for services to assessing need came with the NHS *and Community Care Act*. This required social workers and other assessors to look at what services may have to be purchased or provided in order to enable that individual to live more independently. Sapey (1993) argued that the 1990 Act was a continuation of an ideological tradition within social policy that started with the Poor Laws in that it maintained local authorities, rather than disabled people, know best what is needed by the latter. It would be wrong to focus solely on the practice of the individuals employed, when the policy structure itself demands such behaviour of them.

The problems were two-fold, first was the need to be able to distinguish between the rhetoric and reality of assessment policies and second, that assessments accurately reflect the needs of the client concerned, and not professional commitment, consciously or unconsciously, to one or other model or view of the world.

Recently, the needs-led approach was changed to a requirement for outcome-based assessments and reviews (Department of Health, 2010a). Once desired outcomes are determined then needs are assessed in order to work out the type of support required. So although the assessment starts with considering outcomes it soon reverts to being needs led. In practice, assessments have to fit in with the policy and guidance of *the eligibility framework* first described in *Fair Access to Care Services* (Department of Health, 2003) and referred to again in *Prioritising need in the context of Putting People First* (Department of Health, 2010: 21). Those that may be considered for social care will fall into one of four categories of *critical, substantial, moderate* or *low*; increasingly local authorities have been funding only critical and substantial needs. Another major purpose of assessment is in ascertaining the cost of support:

Eligibility criteria therefore describe the full range of eligible needs that will be met by councils, taking their resources into account. Councils should work with individuals to identify the outcomes they wish to achieve, and to identify where unmet needs are preventing the realisation of such outcomes. (Department of Health, 2010a: 19)

In effect local authorities still decide how needs are met as cost is a major determinant of which services a person will be allowed. Disabled people's fears that cost will be used as the reason for the withdrawal of support were heightened when in the case of *McDonald, R v Royal Borough of Kensington & Chelsea* (2010) the Court of Appeal decision was that local authorities do have the right to withdraw or amend care support where the recipient's circumstances are unchanged. This was found largely because the 'local authority is responsible also for acting on behalf of the interests of all the clients whose welfare it supports with the use of limited resources' (*McDonald, R v Royal Borough of Kensington & Chelsea*, 2010).

Self-assessment

While the problems of poor assessment are easy to identify it is perhaps more difficult to locate a particular model for good practice. Sapey and Hewitt (1991) have argued that social workers and other social services personnel stand between disabled people and their rights derived from various welfare enactments. As the provision of services is dependent on the local authority assessment of need, this places the assessors of that need in a position, not simply of gate-keeping scarce resources, but of sanctioning the rights to services prescribed by parliament. They go on to suggest that if assessments are to be needs led they must also be undertaken by the disabled person. Self-assessment has received some official sanction, for example when drawing up guidelines on working with disabled people, CCETSW argued: 'Self-assessment should be central to the assessment process and subsequent planning and evaluation should start from the same stand-point; in other words, disabled people are the best definers of their own needs' (Stevens, 1991: 19).

The Social Care Institute for Excellence (SCIE) actively promotes self-assessment. At a SCIE seminar on independent living in November 2004, each of the speakers, including those from the Disability Rights Commission and government, made it clear that self-assessment must be the next step to ensure that disabled people have real access to independent living. Self-assessment for some health needs is supported by the Department of Health. Many Local Authorities (for example Lincolnshire, York, Reading) have online self-assessment processes which give an indication of whether someone may be eligible for a complex assessment. However this may simply be a way of filtering out some potential applicants while the 'real' assessment is still carried out by social workers of community care assessors.

Middleton (1997: 3–4) had some concern about self-assessment, but she emphasised that a professional role in assessment must be more than a one-to-one activity that comes up with a plan:

> Assessment is the art of managing competing demands, and negotiating the most reasonable outcome. It means steering between the clashing rocks of organisational demand; legislative dictates; limited resources; political and personal agendas. It includes having to keep one's feet in an inter-agency setting when the ground beneath them is constantly shifting. It is about making sense of the situation as a whole, and working out the best way to achieve change.

Thus assessment and self-assessment are complex tasks which will involve much more than the ticking of boxes on a prescribed form. Middleton's argument is that social workers have much to offer when working in partnership with disabled people. Harris (2004:) argued that if we are to stop processing disabled people into service users, we need to change the focus of assessment from needs as defined by agencies, to outcomes as desired by disabled people. 'There are a number of reasons why focusing upon 'needs' is problematic, both conceptually and practically. The identification of 'needs' is no mean feat, since theoretically these are subjective, potentially endless and relative to one's immediate situation.' (Harris, 2004: 117)

Harris believes the supposed objectivity of professionals creates hierarchical relationships with disabled people who will have a more subjective view of their own needs. Furthermore, as needs change over time and as one need is met, another may materialise, disabled people become locked into a service user role in which they are dependent on the professional assessor. Her argument arises from an attempt to implement a social model approach to assessment through making significant changes to its focus. In this study assessors focus on the outcomes that disabled people want from the services, rather than on a normative view of their needs. In this way needs become self-defined as they arise from the aspirations that disabled people have, not from the responsibilities that local authorities believe they have in deciding to ensure safety and comfort, or to act as arbiters in a 'needs versus wants' debate. This is also an area where CILs can offer peer support from experienced disabled people who are familiar with the issues and procedures in self-assessment.

From a social model perspective, the idea that assessment should be empowering seems clear and receives a lot of support, both in terms of the involvement of disabled people as full participants within the process of assessment, but also in terms of the outcomes. While structural barriers to such an approach may remain, practitioners can nevertheless begin to work in a more participatory way. Good advice on this comes from Morris (1997a; 2002) who first focuses on the skills required by individual practitioners if they are to implement a needs-led assessment in ways that are compatible with the independent living movement and latterly on communication skills. While, Ellis (1993) also highlighted the institutional and attitudinal barriers to user participation, she argued that despite the powerless position professionals may perceive themselves to be in, they do have discretion to choose between competing models of practice in assessment. It is they who will implement the assessment procedures of their agencies and it is they who will reinterpret against the interests of their clients if they so choose. Good practice in assessment will involve a clear understanding of the power dynamics that operate between the social worker and disabled person for these are central to an incorporation of the social model of disability. Thompson (1998) also provides some very practical ways in which social workers can think about how they practise in both oppressive and empowering organisations.

Holdsworth (1991: 27) also argued that the principal outcome of an assessment should be geared to 'needs for empowerment':

> what might be the characteristics of an empowerment model of social work with physically disabled people? Probably the most important of these, having accepted the implications of the social model of disability and the concept of disability as oppression, is the ability to start where the client is, as any individual disabled person could be at any point along a continuum of power and powerlessness and will therefore need *a service geared to her specific needs for empowerment.* (Emphasis added)

While empowerment may be central to the assessment and service provision processes, it is important that it is understood from a social model perspective. For some years now it has become part of the rhetoric of central government, local authorities and the social work profession, and it has reached the point where it is an organising principle for institutional change in the public and private sectors (Baistow, 1995). This does not, however, mean that it will result in any benefit for disabled people, and empowerment is not something that should be thought of as the gift of social workers. Freire (1972) argued that empowerment is a process in which powerless people themselves take power away from the powerful. Social workers are in a position of power, as are their employing agencies and the various levels of government. If social workers have a role to play in the process of disabled people empowering themselves, it will be as allies and as people who are prepared to give up and share their own power.

Assessments that take account of individual and social aspects of disability and the relationship between them need to be undertaken by competent and knowledgeable professionals in collaboration with disabled people to ensure that they take into account the wishes, concerns and goals of their clients. Also, and most importantly, if the social dimension is included, then it is social workers who need to be involved because they are concerned with the tertiary level of intervention which, when approached as an issue of empowerment has the potential to become a primary-level intervention in terms of a social model of disability.

Other social services provision

Managing the different agencies involved in providing funding for their support has been a logistical feat for many disabled people, the divide been health services and social services and the various funding for housing, employment support and disability benefits has involved working with many different agencies. This has been recognised for a long time and in the late 1960s the Seebohm report called for improved coordination between services. The NHS and Community Care Act, 1990 made inter-agency coordination mandatory and the emphasis from the Department of Health changed to one of cooperation. A range of guidelines and circulars were issued advising and instructing social services, health and housing authorities on how to ensure they worked together effectively. Critics, including the Audit Commission, argued that instead of breaking down the barriers to cooperation and coordination, the introduction of market principles created more impermeable boundaries determined by budgetary priorities and responsibilities. Despite this being in place for almost two decades there were still problems and the benefits of joint working are still being explained in social policy guidance from government (Department of Health, 2010b: 15).

As well as improving outcomes for people who use services and their carers, evidence may suggest that joint approaches between health and social care can also reduce demand on both systems. Whilst contributing to longer-term independence and well-being for example, investment in re-ablement and intermediate care can prevent hospital admission or post hospital transfer to long term care, or reduce the level of ongoing home care support required. Social care interventions can lead to reductions in the need for health services, just as health interventions can reduce the need for social care services.

Changes proposed in 2010 mean that local authorities will be taking responsibility for many health services previously provided by Primary Care Trusts – the intention is that this will streamline some support for disabled people. In addition the pilots for *Right to Control* referred to earlier, could simplify coordination.

Community-based services

Disabled people who do not wish to manage their own personal assistance using direct payments may prefer other community based services such as home care, professional support (e.g., occupational therapy), equipment and adaptations, day care, meals and short-term residential care. These may be purchased by local authorities from third sector organisations on behalf of disabled people. Traditionally, voluntary sector provision for disabled people extends from residential and day-care services to providing individual volunteers for gardening, driving people to appointments, and so on. The uncritical cooperation, which was formalised through purchasing contracts since 1993, was extensively criticised by organisations *of* disabled people and CILs which challenged the structures within which welfare has been provided (see Campbell and Oliver, 1996 for a full account of their development).

Overall numbers of people receiving community-based and other support has declined. The NHS Information Centre (2011a: 39) state that the number of service users receiving community-based services during the years 2004/05 to 2009/10 showed a gradual rise during this period and

> the number of service users receiving community based services has decreased by 5 per cent from 1.54 million service users in 2008–09 to 1.46 million in 2009–10. Of those service users receiving community based services, 65 per cent were aged 65 and over. Feedback from councils suggests that this fall is due to a number of technical reasons including data cleaning and changes to recording systems following the introduction of self directed support as well as to the wider use of grant funded services for those with a lower level of need. Councils have reported that there may be a further fall next year as this continues.

The reference to people with lower level of need is related to the tightening of eligibility criteria under Fair Access to Services (FACS), whereby nearly all local authorities provide support only to people who are assessed as having critical or substantial needs, some local authorities have divided the substantial level and fund only upper substantial needs. Local authorities are making more effort to review people's support; if people's circumstances have changed they may be assessed as having low or moderate needs and will therefore not be eligible for support. Some people will probably be correctly moved from substantial or critical category to moderate category at review, however others may be moved even though their circumstances have not changed. They would then be told they are no longer eligible to a support package, and would only be able to retain the support through challenging the decision. The approach is now becoming mechanistic through the Care Funding Calculator (iese, 2011, online) which sets out to save money on care costs. Also local authorities have increased their charges for support which many disabled people find difficult to pay, and so do not take the services they need (Clark, 2006).

Although numbers of people receiving community-based support has decreased the overall expenditure on adult social care has increased suggesting that those receiving support packages have a higher average cost, probably because they have higher support needs.

> Local Authorities have reported an increase in Adult Social Service Gross Current Expenditure from £16.1 billion in 2008–09 to £16.8 billion in 2009–10, this is approximately 5 per cent in cash terms and 3 per cent real terms. Over a longer

term, this represents a real term increase of 10 per cent since 2004–05 and 47 per cent over the 10 years from 1999–[20]00. (NHS Information Centre, 2011b:4)

Traditional administrative divisions have meant that there are different funding streams and levels of service for people in the different groups: older people, people with mental distress, people with learning difficulties, and people with physical and or sensory impairments. The demographic changes in the UK population means that the numbers of older people are increasing every year, older people are the largest group receiving adult social care. This demonstrates a large demand with an estimated 1.22 million (68 per cent) of those receiving services being aged 65 and over (NHS Information Centre, 2011a).

There has been a practice that people are not allowed support in their own home if their personal support needs cost more than a residential home, this is a cause of great worry for disabled people who fear that they will be forced into residential care against their will. A change of attitude may be insufficient in itself to replace the physical legacy of centuries of development of institutions.

Residential accommodation for disabled people: a discredited provision

As already noted the moves toward independent living are slow and limited. It is easy to see how by working within the individual model of disability those involved in planning and providing services for disabled people are led to see residential provision as a suitable option when an individual is no longer able to continue living as before, whether as a consequence of family break up, lack of community support and/or increasing impairment. Dalley (1996) argued that residential care reflects the ideological attitudes of society as to what form care should take at any particular time. It appears however that the application of this ideology may be selective according to medical conditions. This then suggests that people with particular types of impairments may be more vulnerable to being institutionalised, as are older disabled people. Dalley considered however, that staying home was favoured and indeed, there has been a gradual acknowledgement that the most appropriate place to live is in the community, even for those people with considerable impairments.

Although there are more options for disabled people than there were 60 years ago there has been a massive growth in residential provision since 1948 when the NHS inherited just 55,000 beds for chronically sick people from the Poor Law infirmaries and work-houses (Barnes, 1991). This number peaked later in the twentieth century and although it has decreased recently there are still about 215,000 people living in residential homes (NHS Information Centre, 2011a: 33). For those disabled people who do not currently live in residential homes there is the constant fear that if their support package costs more than the cost of a residential home then they may be required to move into a residential home. Over the past few decades there have been fewer younger disabled people living in residential homes (NHS Information Centre, 2011a).

Residential care is the antithesis of independent living for all client groups and has been heavily criticised for years. This is equally true in respect of disabled people who fear that residential care may be the only option available to them if their personal assistant requirement is deemed too costly. From the perspective of the social model of disability, there is little doubt that the experi-ence of residential care further disables people with impairments. In 2008 the United Nations gave support to the right to independ-ent living in the *Convention on the Rights of People with Disabilities*. Article 19 requires countries to ensure that 'Persons with disabilities have the opportunity to choose their place of resi-dence and where and with whom they live on an equal basis with others and are not obliged to live in a particular living arrange-ment' (United Nations, undated: 13).

The UN (undated: 14) also made it clear in Article 14 of the Convention that countries should ensure that 'any deprivation of liberty is in conformity with the law, and that the existence of a disability shall in no case justify a deprivation of liberty'.

While admission to residential homes is not normally made under compulsion as is often the case with psychiatric hospitals, it could be considered de facto compulsion if alternatives are not made available.

Since the publication of *Asylums* (Goffman, 1961) there has been a considerable amount of work on the effects of institutional-isation. 'Total institutions', as Goffman called them, are charac-terised by a loss of privacy, a lack of freedom of choice, and the individual within them misses the opportunity to make meaningful personal relationships. The institution provides a highly structured routine where the lives of the individual residents are regulated by management and all tend to be treated alike. This gives rise to what had earlier been identified as institutional neurosis:

[A] disease characterised by apathy, lack of initiative, loss of interest more marked in things and events not immediately personal or present, submissiveness, and sometimes no expression of feelings or resentment at harsh or unfair orders. There is also a lack of interest in the future and an apparent inability to make practical plans for it, a deterioration in personal habits, toilet and standards generally, a loss of individuality, and a resigned acceptance that things will go on as they are – unchangingly, inevitably and indefinitely. (Barton, 1959: 2)

Studies specifically concerned with institutions for disabled people have tended to see the effects of institutionalisation on the residents in less dramatic terms. The 'warehousing' model of residential care described by Miller and Gwynne (1972) which they called the conventional approach to residential care, approximates to Goffman's total institution in its requirement that the inmate remain dependent and depersonalised and subjugated to the task of the institution. Miller and Gwynne (1972: 87) were 'captured by the plight of intelligent cripples ... who were forced to lead stunted lives in institutions that do not provide opportunities for their development'.

Miller and Gwynne (1972) drew the distinction between 'warehousing' and 'horticultural' models of residential care. The warehousing model expresses the humanitarian or medical value that the prolongation of life is a good thing, but the question concerning the purpose of the life that is prolonged is never asked. The emphasis is on medical care and the minimisation of risk – the main aim is to keep the gap between social death (the point when the disabled person enters the institution) and physical death as long as possible. Alternatively the horticultural model emphasises the uniqueness of each inmate, the importance of individual responsibility and the potential to realise unfulfilled ambitions and capacities.

However, Miller and Gwynne (1972) failed to fully endorse the horticultural model because of their concerns that it was problematic due to the overvaluing of independence, and the distortion of staff–resident relations where the real facts of the situation are ignored or distorted. The formative years of the disabled people's movement saw Paul Hunt and other residents of Le Court realising that regardless of changes that might be made to the operation of residential homes, the process of segregation would continue to be a process of social death that could only be countered by living options that were integrated within the community. Disabled people themselves sought ways of living independently within communities rather than in residential homes:

> In Great Britain we have a habit of providing for 'difficult' minority groups in segregated institutions and those suffering traumatic tetraplegia are no exception. It is a tradition which has roots in the Poor Law and which comes down to us today virtually unchanged. Only rarely can someone who depends heavily on others for personal help, and who for some reason does not have the support of – or wishes to live independently of – his or her family, find an alternative system of accommodation and care. (Davis, 1981: 322)

Many criticisms of residential care implicitly and explicitly draw upon the social model of disability in that they see institutional regimes as adding to, rather than alleviating many of the problems that disabled individuals face. Some, like the UPIAS (1976), called for nothing less than the complete disappearance of all segregated institutions:

> The Union's eventual object is to achieve a situation where as physically impaired people we all have the means to choose where and how we wish to live. This will involve the phasing out of segregated institutions maintained by the State or Charities. (UPIAS, 1975: 4)

The social model shows the way in which disability is imposed upon individuals who have impairments, and so disability is a consequence of the way society is organised. There can be little doubt that residential care disables individuals with impairments, and from this viewpoint residential care offers an unacceptable form of provision.

There has been little recent research concerning younger disabled adults in residential care, if the circumstances of their admission are in any way similar to those of older people, these fears may well be justified. Booth (1992: 2) concluded from a comprehensive review of studies about elderly residents that 'Most people do not themselves make a positive choice to enter residential care, and the majority are admitted (often with little consultation and sometimes under pressure) as the result of arrangements by someone else.'

The continued use of residential care may also be due to personal economic factors. Schorr (1992) pointed to the correlation that exists, in both the United Kingdom and the United States, between the use of residential care and income. It is only when the spending power of older people has increased relative to the incomes of others in the population, that there has been any reduction in the trend of increasing numbers of people entering residential homes. He argued that changes in welfare policy must include income maintenance issues as well as personal social services policy if community care is to succeed. This was also the position taken in 1976 by the Union of Physically Impaired Against Segregation (UPIAS) in its statement of Fundamental Principles of Disability:

> Of course the Union supports and struggles for increased help for physically impaired people, there can be no doubt about our impoverishment and the need for urgent change. However, our Union's Aims seek the 'necessary financial ... and other help required from the State to enable us to gain the maximum possible independence in daily living activities, to achieve mobility, undertake productive work and to live where and how we choose with full control over our lives'. (UPIAS, 1976: 15)

However the financial circumstances of older people is not improving as the reduction in the value of private pensions and superannuation alongside low public pensions is keeping incomes very modest. These trends have important ramifications for the shape and future of residential care facilities for disabled people.

Langan (1990) had argued that community care legislation which encourages the expansion of the independent sector would cause this growth of institutional care as it is more profitable than any of the alternatives. In the twenty-first century there is even more emphasis on the independent sector so the situation could become even worse for disabled people. A small organisation with the intention of supporting improvement of 'residential care' is *The Residential Forum*. *The Residential Forum* it is generally quite positive about the sector, but even here there is acknowledgement that going into 'care' is not often a positive choice, but due to lack of support in the community (2010: online):

- Some older people with various form of physical and mental disability opt for residential care in preference to feeling a burden to relatives and neighbours, or coping alone with failing competence, loss of confidence, feelings of isolation and loneliness, growing anxiety, depression, or confusion.

- Others who would rather not be in residential care, but accept it as inevitable, often come to value the companionship it offers, and resolve to make the best of it.
- Others again feel residential admission has been imposed on them by a lack of viable alternatives, breakdown of family and other support networks, withdrawal of NHS or social services support to stay at home, or pressure from relatives, neighbours, GPs or hospital staff.

The Residential Forum seems to accept the inadequacies of support in the community as a valid reason for people to be in residential homes, even if it is not want they want.

The question for those charged with responsibility for providing personal support when using the individual model of disability automatically becomes: 'what does the individual need?' The answer simplistically is food, clothing, shelter and personal assistance, and when individual needs are aggregated it seems not unreasonable to meet these needs through the provision of residential accommodation for a number of individuals, especially given the social and economic pressures from the care industry to make such a choice.

The question for social workers using the social model, however, is different, and becomes: in what ways does the physical and social environment prevent this individual from remaining in the community, from continuing to live an independent life, and from achieving their aspirations? This obviously produces a different answer along the lines of the basic needs of independent living to include seeking suitable and adequate housing, a reasonable income to ensure access to food, clothing and personal assistance, the provision of community support, and so on.

CHAPTER OVERVIEW
- The aims of the disabled people's movement, and the essential difference of the citizenship approach to welfare provision, are that disabled people should be able to experience the same degree of independent living as any non-disabled person.

- Traditional approaches to welfare including residential care and many of the semi-independent alternatives that we have reviewed fail to provide the same degree of independent living.
- Attempting to improve such services can only ever amount to the treatment of symptoms rather than the cause, which is the use of such services in the first place.
- What is required of social workers is that they first understand the meaning and implications of independent living and second, that they use their skills and their role within the welfare system to support disabled people in pursuit of this.
- While many models of care have been provided over the years, the key to independent living is that full control of the provision of personal assistance should be handed over to the disabled person who is to receive it.
- Within the new market structures of welfare in the United Kingdom this means giving disabled people the finances to resource their own personal assistance schemes and then supporting them in that task in ways that they determine as being of use.
- Social workers make much of their commitment to anti-oppressive practice and their value base, but the body responsible for inspecting their activities describes them as holding 'restrictive or patronising attitudes', of being unaware of what they should be doing or worse, erecting barriers in order to maintain power on the services that disabled people need to use.
- It is clear that autonomy and citizenship can only be achieved by independent living.

Points for reflection

Exercise 1

Direct payments have been considered by many disabled people as the route to independence choice and control, however some are concerned about managing this. What are likely to be the main concerns that people have about managing their own budgets and how could a social worker help them to keep choice and control over their support?

> **Exercise 2**
>
> Respite care is a common provision of social services departments and often takes the form of institutionalising older and disabled people in order to provide their families with a break from caring for them. However, this suggests that the individual in need of support is the source of the problem and that their removal resolves it.
>
> Think creatively about what alternatives you could offer the family carers of: (a) an older person; (b) a person with learning difficulties; and (c) a person with physical impairments. The aim of your alternatives should be to avoid institutionalising one person in order to provide respite to another.

Further resources

Glasby, J. and Littlechild, R. (2009) *Direct payments and personal budgets: Putting personalisation into practice* (Bristol, The Policy Press).
A study of how direct payments work and the barriers created by poor social work practice.

Morris, J. (1993) Independent Lives: *Community Care and Disabled People* (Basingstoke, Macmillan).
A study of the impact of disabled people being able to pay for personal assistance on their own lives.

Priestley, M. (1999) *Disability Politics and Community Care* (London, Jessica Kingsley).
A study of how a disabled people's organisation are able to improve the quality of community care.

Centre for Independent Living, Berkley, California, United States was founded in 1972. This is the first CIL in the world. The website reflects the difference in analysis in United States where they use the term 'people with disabilities'. It works to open doors in the community to full participation and access for all. It was set up, is run and controlled by disabled people: www.cilberkeley.org/

National Centre for Independent Living is a national organisation that promotes choice, control, rights and full economic, social and cultural lives. It was set up and is run and controlled by disabled people: www.ncil.org.uk/

Southampton Centre for Independent Living was established in the mid 1980s one of the first CILs in the UK offering a range of services to support disabled people. It was set up, is run and controlled by disabled people: www.southamptoncil.co.uk/

CHAPTER 5

Independent living: the wider social policy and legal context

Introduction

Earlier chapters have discussed issues of independent living which are mainly related to personal assistance – whether this is managed by the disabled person themselves, organised by a family (or informal) carer, or local authority in the form of domiciliary care or residential care. However independent living is about much more than this, as shown in the development of the 12 rights of independent living discussed in Chapter 4, but there are too many of these to cover in this book. In order to take account of disabled people in this wide-ranging context, a whole-system approach is required. This chapter covers several of these issues in relation to relevant legislation and social policy guidance.

In earlier chapters reference has been made to the landmark social policy of *Putting People First* which was introduced in 2007; from April 2011 this has been replaced with *Think Local, Act Personal*. This is important because its main principle is that of taking a whole community approach and to bring about a cultural change within local authorities so that areas such as employment, housing, education, community safety, information and advice become much more inclusive of disabled people. This is intended to assist in providing early intervention and prevention of dependency on social care, and also to increase choice and control. Taking an inclusive whole community approach should assist disabled people in taking an active role in local communities and they should then have social capital – that is they become valued for their contribution, have reciprocal relationships and are part of networks (Think Local, Act Personal, 2011). However the policy of taking a whole system approach is not as prominent in *Think Local, Act Personal* as it was in *Putting People First*, thus diverting attention away from societal systems structures that do not take account of disabled people and thus excludes them.

Legislation and social policy, whether specific to disabled people or general, often does not take account of people with impairments, or it totally misunderstands the issues, thus disabling them.

Some of the legal measures taken to combat exclusion and disadvantage actually further contribute to the disabling process. Earlier chapters have referred to some of the legislation and social policy in this respect and this chapter focuses upon some aspects of the relationship between disabled people and society and considers some of the possible intervention strategies for social workers.

While it is possible to trace state involvement and concern with disabled people back to 1601 and beyond (Borsay, 2005 takes it back to 1247) there is little need to go back further than the 1940s when the foundations of the welfare state were laid. Prior to this, statutory provision for disabled people had been made on a piecemeal or ad hoc basis and often only related to specific types of impairment or the way in which impairments had been caused. While this specificity has not been completely eradicated, state provision is now geared towards disabled people as a single group. It is interesting that employment has been the focus of much of this legislation, indicating its importance in ensuring inclusion in mainstream society.

Employment

Employment is critical to the way in which our society is organised, but the dominant social perception of disabled people is as 'dependent' and not able to work because of their personal functional limitations:

> Disability itself has come to mean 'unable to work' and as non-earners disabled people are now fundamentally identified as incapable home makers and unsuitable love partners. (Finkelstein 1991: 29)

However, a social model perspective moves the focus to the way in which work is organised in modern society:

> The world of work (buildings, plant, machinery, processes and jobs, practices, rules, even social hierarchies) is geared to able-bodied people, with the objective of maximising profits. The growth of large-scale industry has isolated and excluded disabled people from the processes of production, in a society which is work centred. (Swain, 1981: 11–12)

This is crucial in late capitalist society, where individuals are still judged upon what their job is, and appropriate social status thereby accorded. Roulstone and Warren (2006: 117) use what they call a barriers approach in considering employment from a social model perspective:

> The now well recorded labour market barriers faced by disabled people in accessing paid work are reflected in studies detailing the internal organisational, physical and attitude barriers that limit disabled people's job and career prospects.

For most people employment is their main or only source of income, it provides a purpose in life and it is part of their identity and status. This indicates how not being in employment, or being perceived as being unable to work can have a profound negative effect on disabled people.

The Disabled Persons (Employment) Act, 1944

The first Act of Parliament to treat disabled people as one single category was the *Disabled Persons (Employment) Act, 1944*. It provided a framework for the provision of a variety of employment rehabilitation and resettlement services. Alongside the numerous day centres and Adult Training Centres run by social services and health authorities, the Department of Employment operated up to 27 rehabilitation centres at their peak in the 1980s. The 1944 Act also gave disabled people legal rights to employment, in that it placed an obligation on all employers with more than 20 workers to employ a quota of 3 per cent of the workforce who were registered as disabled, but in practice this was never enforced and disabled people continued to experience a higher level of unemployment than non-disabled people.

The *Disability Discrimination Act*, 1995, The *Disability Discrimination Act*, 2005, and the *Equality Act*, 2010

The 1944 Act was repealed by part II of the *Disability Discrimination Act, 1995* which replaced the quota system and registration of disabled people in favour of defining lawful and unlawful discrimination in employment. However the concept of being 'registered disabled' remains even though there is no such register. Since December 1996 it has been unlawful for businesses and organisations to treat disabled people less favourably than other people for a reason related to their disability and since October 1999 they have had to make reasonable adjustments for disabled people, such as providing extra help, making changes to the organisation of jobs and to the way they provide services to customers, including from 2004 making reasonable adjustments to the physical features of their premises to overcome barriers to access. Services here include social work and social care services, in addition public bodies have a duty to promote disability equality and rather than simply react to individuals requiring reasonable adjustments, they must consider the impact of their actions and avoid creating disabling barriers.

The *Equality Act 2010* has now replaced the Disability Discrimination Acts, but continues with those same requirements. Enforcement remains a problem since the law relies on individuals taking cases against their employer or potential employer.

Despite these measures, which are intended to get disabled people into work, the figures are very similar to a decade ago. Only 40 per cent of disabled people of working age are in work, of the rest 25 per cent wish to be in work, the remaining 35 per cent do not want to work or are not well enough to work. Among those who are aged 25 to retirement and are not working, almost half are disabled (The Poverty Site, 2011: online).

Further information from the Labour Force survey (Palmer, 2011: online) shows that disability affects people's access to employment more than gender or being a lone parent. In 2010:

- The work rates for those who are neither disabled nor a lone parent are around 80 per cent for women and 90 per cent for men. By contrast, work rates for disabled, non-lone parents are around 40 per cent for both men and women.
- Lone parenthood reduces the female employment rate by 15 percentage points (from 80 per cent to 65 per cent), disability reduces employment for both female lone parents and female non-lone parents by around 35 percentage points and 40 percentage points (from 65 per cent to 30 per cent and 80 per cent to 40 per cent respectively).
- At every level of qualification, the proportion of people aged 25 to 49 with a work-limiting disability who lack, but want, paid work is much greater than for those without a disability.

Unemployment is often the major problem that many disabled people face, those that do find employment are often in less skilled jobs, earning lower wages than their non-disabled counterparts. The importance of employment was recognised in *Improving the Life Chances of Disabled People* (Prime Minister's Strategy Unit,

2005) as was the importance of welfare services in helping disabled people in this respect. The role of GPs in offering help was incorporated into the 2006 *White Paper, Our Health Our Care Our Say* (Department of Health, 2006: 29).

Although social workers have frequently questioned whether it is part of the social work task to attempt to alleviate such problems, if employment is assessed as the major problem they should take a more active role. This role was emphasised in the third national objective of *Modernising Social Services* in 1998. Social workers who are working with unemployed disabled people should be prepared to see the provision of services and support required to help someone find a job as part of their task. This includes putting them in touch with agencies that offer support in finding work. For example, support is offered to young people through Connexions, which provides information and advice about employment. The Job Centre Plus will help disabled adults, who may have difficulties in finding suitable employment, to become more employable through offering training to improve skills and practical support. However, their effectiveness could be enhanced if social workers are prepared to work in an advocacy role with disabled people, rather than simply seeing employment as the responsibility of these other agencies.

This may be given low budgetary priority so social workers need to be imaginative and practical about how they help, ensuring that their own employers meet their obligations as well as criticising others who fail to do so. This would involve ensuring the agency does not have disabling barriers which effectively stop disabled people from gaining and maintaining a job. Social workers can also advocate good practice within their own organisations which may have a tendency to view disabled people as dependent clients rather than potential employees.

Income

Disabled people's exclusion from the work force is bound to have an impact on income and the history of the disabled people's movement involved much discussion and disagreement about welfare benefits starting in the 1970s when both the Disablement Income Group and the Disability Alliance put forward proposals that the main cause of disabled people exclusion was the lack of a national disability income as of right. The Union of the Physically Impaired Against Segregation (UPIAS) suggested that poverty was a symptom of disabled people's oppression and not the cause, and consequently it may be inappropriate to attack the symptom without dealing with the cause. UPIAS (1976: 3) advanced three fundamental principles when considering disability to be:

a social situation, caused by social conditions, which requires for its elimination

(a) that no one aspect such as incomes, mobility, or institutions is treated in isolation,

(b) that disabled people should, with the help and advice of others, assume control over their own lives, and

(c) that professionals, experts and others who seek to help must be committed to promoting such control by disabled people.

However disabled people continue to have lower incomes than non-disabled people and there continues to be considerable debate about how this might be changed.

At the time of writing in 2011 the welfare benefits system has been undergoing a major overhaul, the Welfare Reform Bill is making its way through Parliament with the government making some strong claims about what it will achieve. However, a strong feature of their approach is to reduce expenditure on benefits by placing more responsibility for poverty on individuals.

The main elements of the Welfare Reform Bill (Department for Work and Pensions, 2011: online) are:

- the introduction of Universal Credit to provide a single streamlined benefit that will ensure work always pays;
- a stronger approach to reducing fraud and error with tougher penalties for the most serious offences;
- a new claimant commitment showing clearly what is expected of claimants while giving protection to those with the greatest needs;
- reforms to Disability Living Allowance, through the introduction of the Personal Independence Payment to meet the needs of disabled people;
- creating a fairer approach to Housing Benefit to bring stability to the market and improve incentives to work;
- driving out abuse of the Social Fund system by giving greater power to local authorities;
- reforming Employment and Support Allowance to make the benefit fairer and to ensure that help goes to those with the greatest need; and

- changes to support a new system of child support which puts the interest of the child first.

This approach has caused disabled people much worry and fear that they will lose the finance that goes some way toward covering the cost of impairment and disability; for some of those who are in receipt of the Disability Living Allowance it makes the difference between being able to working and not.

It could be argued that as financial benefits fall within the province of the Department for Work and Pensions (DWP) social workers should not get involved. However, there are two arguments that can counter this: it is clear that the (DWP) cannot be relied on to ensure that disabled people get their entitlements; and as poverty is a major problem for many disabled people, it is an abrogation of professional responsibility not to make any attempt to alleviate it. Both individual welfare rights advice, provided it is accurate, and the establishment of welfare rights projects, are thus part of the social work task. Involvement in the incomes approach to disability can be viewed as a personal or political rather than professional responsibility, and while social workers may join organisations in their spare time, active involvement in the politics of disability might be considered beyond their professional duty. The difficulty with this position however, is that it involves sitting on the fence which has the effect of supporting the *status quo*, which in turn implies support for the continuation of policies that leave disabled people in poverty.

For the social worker, who is working with a disabled person whose poverty is current, immediate action is necessary and social workers have a record of being effective advocates when they do help their clients with benefits issues. In order to minimise poverty and reduce economic disability, it is important that disabled people receive all the benefits to which they are entitled. Some professionals believe myths such as 'you can't get the attendance component if you work', or 'you can't get the mobility component if you can walk'. In order to make sure that the disabled people they are working with receive the entitled benefits they are entitled to social workers should keep themselves informed and up to date by having the *Disability Rights Handbook* (which is produced every year by the Disability Alliance) to hand. It is the simplest yet most accurate and comprehensive guide to welfare benefits, both social workers and disabled people can use it. This, along with the Internet, will keep social workers up-to-date with the tribunal and court rulings that may have relevance for disabled people who have previously had claims rejected.

If more expert advice is needed then the Disability Alliance or other local organisations like Disability Information and Advice Line (DIAL) may be able to help, not just with information, but also possibly with representation at appeals or tribunals. Many Local Authorities also have their own welfare benefits maximisation teams, but they may be focussed only on those disabled people who may be required to pay charges for services from the Local Authority, since the Authority can then take at least part of any awards in charges. If there is nothing available locally, social workers could work with disabled people to set up a disability rights project where a number of disabled people in a particular area or day centre are assessed by welfare rights experts to see whether they are getting all that they are entitled to. A longer-term solution involves working with established disabled people's organisations, Centres of Independent Living (CILs) and user-led organisations as discussed in Chapter 4.

Equality and human rights

The era of the very late twentieth century and early twenty-first century saw changes in the welfare system that reflected the concurrent changes around notions of rights and citizenship. The influence of the social model of disability was officially recognised:

> In the field of disability, the development of the 'social model of disability' began to change the way in which people thought about equality in relation to disabled people. This has led to a growing understanding that disadvantages faced by disabled people comes not so much from their particular impairment, but more from the way that society creates disability through physical, systemic, cultural and attitudinal barriers. This meant that campaigning efforts shifted from a focus on a disabled person's particular impairment(s) to the action that should be taken to remove barriers faced by disabled people in everyday life. (Philips, 2007: 34)

The *Disability Discrimination Act, 1995* was the first legislation to officially recognise discrimination against disabled people, but it fell short of disabled people's expectations. One of the major problems identified by disabled people was that the definition of disability was based on the individual model. Another major problem was the concept of 'reasonable' and that discrimination could be 'justified', making it legal to discriminate. This last point was removed with the *Disability Discrimination Act, 2005* which also brought a requirement for public bodies, including statutory social services, to promote disability equality. This duty is also enshrined in the *Equality Act, 2010* which replaces earlier anti-discrimination legislation including the Disability Discrimination Acts of 1995 and 2005.

The definition of disability used in the *Disability Discrimination Act, 1995* referred to people who qualified for legal protection as someone who has a mental or physical impairment that has an adverse effect on their ability to carry out normal day-to-day activities. The adverse effect has to be substantial and long-term and this means at least 12 months. Additionally, several medical conditions were specified without the qualification of adverse effects. However, as this gave people certain rights, contesting whether someone is disabled became the first line of defence of many people whose actions have been challenged under the Act (Gooding, 2003). Although more medical conditions were included in the *Disability Discrimination Act, 2005* and the *Equality Act 2010* the definition of disability is still based on the individual model of disability, 'a physical or mental impairment and the impairment has a substantial and long-term adverse effect on their ability to perform normal day-to-day activities' (Disability Discrimination, undated: online). It is likely that the problems identified by Gooding (2003) about the definition, which allows employers to successfully defend themselves by arguing that the individuals concerned are not disabled people, are likely to remain.

The *Equality Act 2010* covers nine protected characteristics some of them apply to everyone, for example gender, age and race. Other protected characteristics do not apply to all, for example, disability applies to disabled people, but not to non-disabled people. It includes a public duty to anticipate the requirements of people with any of the protected characteristics. In relation to disabled people this means that all public bodies such as local authorities need to be outcome focussed, anticipate the requirements of disabled people and to take action to equalise the situation between disabled people and non-disabled people.

The Act (Equality and Human Rights Commission, 2010: 5) helpfully explains that having regard for advancing equality involves:

- Removing or minimising disadvantages suffered by people due to their protected characteristics.
- Taking steps to meet the needs of people from protected groups where these are different from the needs of other people.
- Encouraging people from protected groups to participate in public life or in other activities where their participation is disproportionately low.

The Act states that meeting different needs involves taking steps to take account of disabled people's disabilities.

European Convention and the Human Rights Act 1998

The European Convention on Human Rights was incorporated into British domestic legislation in 2000 through the *Human Rights Act*, 1998. This provides simpler access to redress under the Convention and places a range of obligations on public bodies, including the employers of most social workers. This has meant that people can take human rights cases, which fall under the European Convention of Human Rights, to UK courts rather than have to go to a European Court.

Under the Convention people have fundamental human rights and freedoms. Some are particularly relevant to disabled people who receive services, such as the right to a private life, to have one's home respected, to have the right to marry and to have a family life. Article 8 of the European Convention, which is the right to a private life, has been particularly relevant to disabled people and some have used the Human Rights Act in this respect, for example: *Rachel Gunter (by her litigation friend and father Edwin Gunter) v South Western Staffordshire Primary Care Trust* (2005):

A disabled woman who required 24 hour care wanted to be cared for at home with her family, through an extensive care package. However, her local Primary Care Trust (PCT) wanted to place her in residential care due to the high cost of home care, and because of the higher quality of care in the residential care home in the event of a crisis. The High Court found that the PCT had not properly considered the impact of this on her family life. They had not taken into account her improved quality of life at home, or her own wishes to be placed at home. The PCT was therefore told to remake their decision, taking her right to respect for her family life into account. (Equality and Human Rights Commission, 2011: online)

In order to receive the support they need to lead an independent life disabled people may have many professional and support staff in their lives who may be a constant presence. Maintaining intimate relationships, friendships and a family life is far more difficult with high levels of support, but can be done far more effectively in one's own home than in a residential institution or nursing home.

In another example Mrs Bernard, who has a mobility impairment, was living in a house that was inaccessible to her. She was assessed by the local authority social services department as requiring more suitable accommodation, but this was not provided and she took action using the Human Rights Act:

> Article 8 placed an obligation on the Council to take positive steps, including the provision of suitably adapted accommodation, to enable Mrs Bernard and her family to enjoy their family life. The court said that suitably adapted accommodation was important not only because it would facilitate family life (for example enabling Mrs Bernard to move around her home more freely and help to look after her children) but also because such accommodation would secure her 'physical and psychological integrity', which is protected by Article 8 (right to family and private life). The court said 'In short it would have restored her dignity as a human being'. The court also awarded Mrs Bernard £10,000 damages under the Human Rights Act. (British Institute of Human Rights, 2011: online)

These examples show the important role that social workers have in ensuring that disabled people are not denied basic rights that non-disabled people take for granted. Clements and Read (2003) argue that good practice in respect of the *Human Rights Act* should not simply follow a checklist of what must be done as a minimum, but that practitioners and their employers should seek to provide best practice by working towards the spirit of the Convention.

UN Convention on the Rights of Persons with Disabilities (CRPD)

In 2006 the United Nations agreed what has been described as a landmark convention, the CRDP. At the time of writing this had been ratified by 99 countries, including the United Kingdom and had been signed by 147 of the 192 member states (http://treaties.un.org). The CRPD covers adults and children and seeks to guarantee all disabled people the right to equality and to be free from discrimination. It recognises the rights of disabled people to access the built-environment, to access education and employment and to participate in political, cultural and social life. It also makes it clear that all people have the right to recognition before the law, to access justice and to be free from abuse. In addition, the UN recognised the right of disabled people to live independently in the community and to have an adequate standard of living:

> Perhaps as important as the enumeration of these specific rights, however, are the underlying values embraced by the Convention. The Convention represents a paradigm shift away from the medical model of disability, which views people with disabilities as sick and in need of a cure. Instead, the Convention adopts a human rights model, which views people with disabilities as rights holders and members of our respective societies who are often more disabled by the physical and attitudinal barriers societies erects to exclude and stigmatize them than by their own physical or mental condition. (Kanter, 2007: 291)

Due to the CRPD, in 2008 the Special Rapporteur of the UN Human Rights Council submitted a report to the General Assembly on *Torture and Other Cruel, Inhuman or Degrading Treatment or Punishment*, which included a comprehensive report in relation to the treatment of disabled people. In his report, Nowak (2008: 8–9) expressed concern that disabled people

> are often segregated from society in institutions, including prisons, social care centres, orphanages and mental health institutions. They are deprived of their liberty for long periods of time including what may amount to a lifelong experience, either against their will or without their free and informed consent. Inside these institutions, persons with disabilities are frequently subjected to unspeakable indignities, neglect, severe forms of restraint and seclusion, as well as physical, mental and sexual violence. The lack of reasonable accommodation in detention facilities may increase the risk of exposure to neglect, violence, abuse, torture and ill-treatment.

For social workers it is important that they recognise and understand the concerns that the UN has about the institutions which disabled people are using on a daily basis. Such segregation is often repackaged as benevolence, protection and necessary respite for carers. However, as the CRDP makes clear, disabled people have the right to receive the resources required to live independently. In a developed nation such as the United Kingdom, there is no economic justification for denying people these rights. The CRDP can be used by social workers working from a social model perspective to reinforce their arguments with budget holders for the provision of independent living services.

Housing

In order to live independently it is self-evident that disabled people need a home of their own and that it should be fully accessible to them, yet finding a suitable home in the owner-occupier sector remains a major barrier for many disabled people (Hemingway, 2011; P. Thomas, 2004). Most studies about housing relate to the social sector with little about owner occupation. There is still the notion of housing (that is 'normal' housing) while accessible housing is considered to be 'adapted' whether it is designed to be accessible or whether it has actually been adapted. This comes from the concept of 'special needs' which unhelpfully marks out disabled people as 'other' rather than mainstream (BCODP, 1987; MacFarlane and Laurie, 1996; Stewart *et al.*, 1999).

Equally adapting a current or new home is problematic. Most homes are difficult and expensive to adapt, eligibility for Disabled Facilities Grants is difficult to obtain and there is evidence that officials exercise their judgements in a subjective manner, which does not allow a fair application and completion process (Sapey, 1995; Thomas and Ormerod, 2005).

Housing developers are required to only abide by Part M of the building regulations that provides facilities for disabled people to visit, but not necessarily to live in the property. Developers have been reluctant to provide even this minimal level of accessibility (Imrie, 2003).

Design standards for housing that allow homes to be easily adapted, if needs change, have been available for well over a decade. These are known as Lifetime Home Standards and they are used in Social Housing, but have been fiercely resisted by private developers. The universal use of Lifetime Homes Standards would reduce any notion of 'special needs' and make considerable budget savings on adaptations since they would become much simpler and therefore less costly.

The Supporting People programme

The Supporting People programme was introduced in April 2003. It provides housing related support in the social sector. Funding has come from a central government formula grant to local authorities, however this is no longer ring fenced and cash strapped local authorities are using non-ringed fenced funding to cover other costs.

In the late 1990s, legal concerns were raised about the use of Housing Benefit to fund rents that included more than the 'bricks and mortar' costs of housing. Many sheltered and supported housing schemes for a wide range of people had included the costs of support in their rents. Before the full programme Supporting People was set up as a project 1998 and in each local area social services and housing authorities formed partnerships that delivered the service. In practice, what happens to people in supported housing is that they receive the bricks and mortar element of their rent from Housing Benefit, and the care is paid for through Supporting People. Both are of course means tested.

However, Watson *et al.* (2003) emphasised that the government appear to have been motivated to use this opportunity to increase the amount and the effectiveness of services for marginalised groups although, they also warn that underfunding of the service, problems related to tenure and a failure so far to reach some of the most marginalised people may undermine these aims. However, as noted earlier, the numbers of older people living in residential or nursing homes has been reducing and it may be that in many parts of the United Kingdom, local policies to use Supporting People to provide more specialised support in social rented housing may be having some effect.

Disabled children and education

Children Act 1989 and 2004

Services for disabled children are provided under the *Children Act, 1989* and although it still uses the individual definition of disability from the *National Assistance Act 1948*, it does mean that children are no longer subject to the restricted list of services that appeared in the 1970 Act, They can expect that:

Every local authority shall provide services designed –

- to minimise the effect on disabled children within their area of their disabilities; and
- to give such children the opportunity to lead lives which are as normal as possible. (*Children Act, 1989*, Schedule 2, Part 1, Section 6)

Despite its use of the term 'normal', which is indicative of the influence of the individual model of disability, the Act opened up the possibility of services that are innovative and relevant to the removal of disabling barriers. The inclusion of disabled children in this Act should ensure that they are not treated differently to other children, but there are difficulties in that Local Authorities with Social Services responsibilities have not always dealt with all children together and this affects their concept of normal. Responsibility for services for disabled children have moved from teams primarily concerned with disability issues to children's teams, which are primarily concerned with child protection and it inevitably this has meant the marginalisation of disability issues. Middleton (1995) suggested that this was made worse by the separate Department of Health guidance on working with disabled children. This allowed disinterested social workers to remain detached. Both managers and practitioners need to ensure that the statutory responsibilities towards disabled children are taken seriously if they are to contribute to the removal of disabling barriers and the promotion of inclusive services (Middleton, 1997). The marginalisation of such services is oppressive and part of the process of disabling children that the *Children Act* sought to minimise. More recently there has been a programme that is intended to improve the situation for disabled children. The *Aiming High for Disabled Children* (AHDC) programme was launched in May 2007 by the Department for Education, It is has three priority areas. First, *access and empowerment* and second, *responsive services and timely support*, both of which are similar in principle to *Thinking Local, Acting Personal*. The change in culture of handing over choice and control to disabled children and their families will need to happen alongside changes that make mainstream services more inclusive. The third priority of *improving quality and capacity* will require real change in leisure services and youth services because access to short breaks has been something that parents have given priority to (Department for Education, 2011b). Although little is known of how the children and young people feel about this, a small research project by Thomas and Clark (2010b) shows that traditional short-break facilities are not wanted. Children and young people choose mainstream facilities. The government is providing specific funding for short breaks and the option of direct payments mean that families are likely to reject traditional facilities and simply go to the places everyone else goes to for a break.

Around 21 per cent (1.6m) of pupils were considered to have Special Education Needs (SEN) in 2010, an increase from 19 per cent (1.53m) in 2006. Not all have statements of SEN and this decreased in 2010 to 220,890 from 236,750 in 2006 (Department for Education, 2010a: 5). Most children who are considered to have SEN have autism, moderate learning difficulties, or considered to have behavioural or communication problems. Only around 20 per cent have physical or sensory impairments (Department for Education, 2010a:13).

The *Education Act, 1944*

The *Education Act, 1944* laid a duty on local authorities to provide education for all children between the ages of 5 and 15 years, and to have regard: 'to the need for securing that provision is made for pupils who suffer from any disability of the mind and body by providing, either in special schools or otherwise, special educational treatment'.

The Act was important for disabled children and their families in that it gave them legal rights to education, but unfortunately it left it to the authorities and to professionals to determine exactly what kind of education was appropriate. It also obliged the authorities to ascertain the numbers of children in their areas who required special educational treatment. The *Special Educational Needs (Information Act) 2008* required the Secretary of State to publish information about children in England with special educational needs to help improve the well-being of these children.

Even more unfortunate was the fact that responsible authorities chose to make provision for the special needs of disabled children in segregated establishments of one kind or another. Despite mounting criticism of special education over many years, both on the grounds of its failure to provide an adequate or comparable education to that provided in ordinary schools, and the social implications of segregating large numbers of children from their peers, the percentage of the school population in special schools grew steadily and is still higher than it was 60 years ago.

The *Warnock Report* in 1978 made numerous recommendations, including a broader concept of 'special educational needs' and the government issued a White Paper in 1980 called *Special Needs in Education*. Warnock, the White Paper and the subsequent *Education Act, 1981* favoured the idea of integration, it made no extra resources available to facilitate such a move. The 1981 Act left the legal rights of parents and their disabled children unchanged and it was left to the local authority to decide on the appropriate educational provision.

The *Education Act, 1993*

The *Education Act, 1993* required local education authorities to accept parental preference for a particular school. However, it left the final decision with the local authority if they either found it would be unsuitable to the individual's special educational needs, incompatible to the education of other children or incompatible with the use of resources (Braye and Preston-Shoot, 1997). The influence of the individual model of disability in which the disabled child is seen as being the problem and the disabled child's exclusion from mainstream schooling as the solution is clear sets boundaries around what might be achieved in changing the environment of education.

There are important implications in the continued commitment to special schools, for, as Tomlinson shows, this is not based solely on the humanitarian ideal of providing what is best for disabled children, but also 'to cater for the needs of ordinary schools, the interests of the wider industrial society and the specific interests of professionals' (Tomlinson, 1982: 57). Indeed, in October 1997 when launching the white paper, *Excellence for all Children*, David Blunkett, then Secretary of State for Education and Employment, made clear his opposition to segregated education and announced his intention to reduce the numbers of children in special schools. The initial response of National Association of Schoolmasters and Union of Women Teachers was to threaten 'not to teach' certain children if integration was to go 'too far'. It is simply unimaginable that such a threat would ever be made on the basis of gender, religion, race or virtually any other characteristic of children, but it was largely accepted as a responsible position in relation to disability. Indeed, while race and sex discrimination laws apply to education, it was specifically excluded from the provisions of the *Disability Discrimination Act, 1995* at that time.

The *Special Educational Needs and Disability Act, 2001*

The *Special Educational Needs and Disability Act, 2001*, amended the Disability Discrimination Act, 1995, and prohibited 'all schools from discriminating against disabled children in their admissions arrangements, in the education and associated services provided by the school for its pupils or in relation to exclusions from the school' (Department for Education and Skills, 2001: v).

The move has been towards an inclusive approach to education in which all schools are expected to be accessible. This is an anticipatory duty where barriers are removed in order that all children should be able to go to the school of their family's choice.

It could be argued that all this is of little relevance to social work. However, more and more parents want their children to be educated in ordinary schools, and in order to achieve those demands against the opposition of vested interests, talked about by Tomlinson (1982), then the parents will need help. Mortier *et al.* (2011: 218) argues strongly from a European perspective.

> Children should have the chance to evolve from being only a recipient of supports to becoming an agent in their own supports. Learning how and being allowed to direct supports will be an essential element of their quality of life and self-determination in childhood as well as in adult life. This will require a balancing act and negation space to (re)define what is appropriate for the child to determine, and what is the responsibility of the adult in the education of this child.

Parents and children will perhaps need advocates to intercede on their behalf and argue that it is not in the best interests of the child, either educationally or socially, that he or she be deprived of family life and links with peers and community for substantial periods during the formative years. Too often the voice of the child or young person themselves goes unheard (Gibson, 2006). Social workers may be ideally placed, by virtue of their regular contact since the birth of the disabled child, to help families negotiate with the education authorities. At present it seems that they are reluctant to take on this advocacy role and to challenge decisions made by their local authority colleagues.

Since the 1970s disabled people, many of whom who have survived the segregated provision of special schools, have campaigned for inclusive education. It is generally accepted in relation to faith and ethnicity that segregation militates against inclusion, yet disabled children and young people are often denied the experience of mixing with non-disabled children and vice versa. Non-disabled children become the adults who see disabled people as an 'other' and consider it quite reasonable to exclude disabled people. Some ground had been gained in this, and mainstream schools have become more welcoming, but it is clear that not all mainstream schools have been offering the necessary support (O'Connell, 2005).

Support and aspiration – Green Paper 2011

For quite some time increasing numbers of parents have demanded the social right to a mainstream education for their children, but it is a hard battle to ensure their child is given an inclusive education with the right support. It is unsurprising that some give up and come to the conclusion that it is easier to opt for a segregated education. Parents of disabled children are just as likely as anyone else to accept that the individual model of disability is obvious and may truly believe that segregation is the best thing for their children. Runswick Cole (2008: 179) found that:

> A social model analysis seems to suggest that parents who lean towards individualised or medicalised models of disability are more likely to choose special schools, whereas those who focus more on barriers to learning, rather than within-child factors, will choose mainstream schools, at least at the beginning of their children's education.

She adds that the process toward inclusion is fragile and this is demonstrated in 2011, when despite the best efforts of parents and disabled people for over 40 years, other vested interests are coming to the fore once again (Department for Education, 2011a). In recognising the problems faced by parents in 2011 the government issued a green paper for consultation, *Support and Aspiration: A New Approach to Special Educational Needs and Disability* noted (Department for Education, 2011a: 51):

> Some parents report that they have little choice in reality because they are not clear about their options, because their local mainstream schools are not able to offer appropriate provision for their child, or because there is a shortage of special school places locally.

Rather than improving mainstream schools the retrograde suggestion is that inclusion is biased:

There should be real choice for parents and that is why we are committed to removing any bias towards inclusion that obstructs parent choice and preventing the unnecessary closure of special schools. We believe that real choice for parents requires a diverse and dynamic school system that offers a wide range of high quality provision and that has the autonomy and flexibility to respond effectively to parental choice; parents to be able to express a preference for a placement in any state-funded school; and good quality information that enables parents to make informed choices. (Department for Education, 2011a: 51)

However the green paper does seem to have some positive points, but how these will be interpreted remains to be seen.

- parents have the option of personalised funding by 2014 to give them greater control over their child's support, with trained key workers helping them to navigate different services;
- parents have access to transparent information about the funding which supports their child's needs;
- parents of disabled children continue to have access to a short break from caring while their child enjoys activities with their peers;
- parents have a clear choice of school; and
- if local authorities and parents disagree, they always try mediation first, to resolve problems in a less adversarial way than having to take their case to the Tribunal. (Department for Education, 2011a: 41–2)

Parents of disabled children do not necessarily understand the long-term implications of segregation and may be relieved at how much easier it seems to be to keep their child away from the mainstream. However, that child will not have the same opportunities to learn how to live in the mainstream world, including the all important social skills and building of social networks and social capital.

The point at which disabled young people move on from school years to adulthood is known among professionals as 'transition'. Families who have fought for the best for their disabled child may be shocked at how much harder it is once their child becomes an adult, particularly if they have not been included in mainstream school and find they are not prepared for what lies ahead. Disabled young people who have been in special schools may find it hard to develop the social skills and networks they need, or they may remain segregated for the rest of their lives.

The rights of disabled people: Ways forward?

It is clear then that disabled people do currently have certain limited rights not to be discriminated against in the employment market, to education commensurate with need, and to a whole range of benefits and services. However, it is plain that many disabled people do not get these rights and there are long-term arguments about how best the rights of disabled people should be safeguarded and extended. These arguments have been characterised as 'persuasion versus enforcement' or 'the carrot versus the stick' (M. Oliver, 1982). The persuasionist view suggests that discrimination against disabled people arises as the result of either negative attitudes or the failure to consider particular 'special' needs. From this point of view what is needed is more information, public education campaigns and research.

The enforcement view, on the other hand, suggests that strong legal action is necessary, for it is only then that disabled people will achieve their rights. There are three problems with this view, 30 years ago it was noted that:

(a) Even if legislation is passed, it may not be enforced – the Disabled Persons (Employment) Act 1944 is a good example of this.

(b) Even if legislation is passed and enforced, it may not achieve its aim of ending discrimination. Both the Equal Pay and Race Relations Acts are examples of this.

(c) Such legislation tends to operate to the benefit of certain sections of the professional classes rather than serve to protect the interests of all the groups for whom the legislation was designed. (M. Oliver, 1982: 78)

This is still the case today and the Disability Discrimination Acts of 1995 and 2005 could be added to the list of examples. Disabled People's Organisations and Centre's of Independent Living could offer a way forward in working with social workers to make whole system changes.

CHAPTER OVERVIEW

- In order for disabled people to live independently and have choice and control over their own lives a whole system approach is required, focussing on one issue alone will not bring about the required changes.
- Employment is a fundamental issue for disabled people as individuals who are the largest group of those unemployed but who want to work.
- Legislation which is intended to alleviate exclusion significantly fails to make much difference, with only a few exceptions.
- Disabled people are over represented in those living in poverty.
- The welfare benefits system has been problematic, but the current reform may leave disabled people in even worse poverty.
- Disabled children are excluded in the education system and this can be a major contributor to exclusion for the rest of their lives.

Points for reflection

Exercise 1

Visit the Equality and Human Rights Commission website at www.equalityhumanrights.com and read about the duties your organisation (employer, university, etc.) has under the Equality Act 2010. With this information, evaluate whether your organisation is meeting its duties by considering what barriers would exist to a disabled person occupying your role. (If you are disabled then consider what barriers would exist to someone with different access needs.)

Exercise 2

List the services that are available for disabled children in your locality and using the three approaches to welfare described in Chapter 1 – Humanitarian, Compliance and Citizenship – determine whether these contribute or detract from disabled children achieving citizenship as compared to non-disabled children.

Further resources

Roulstone, A. and Warren, J. (2006) 'Applying a Barriers Approach to Monitoring Disabled People's Employment: Implications for the Disability Discrimination Act 2005', *Disability & Society*, 21(2): 115–31.
This gives a social model approach to understanding disabled people's exclusion from the workplace.

Thomas, P. (2004) 'The Experience of Disabled People as Customers in the Owner Occupation Market', *Housing Studies*, 19(5): 781–94.
Discusses design barriers experienced by disabled people attempting to buy their own home.

Alliance for Inclusive Education is a national campaigning and information-sharing network led by disabled people: www.allfie.org.uk/

Equality and Human Rights Commission has a statutory remit to promote and monitor human rights; and to protect, enforce and promote equality for people with protected characteristics under the Equality Act 2010: www.equalityhumanrights.com/

Lifetime Homes shows how all new homes can be flexible enough to accommodate individuals and family through changing need that can come about through acquiring impairments: www.lifetimehomes.org.uk/

CHAPTER 6

Independent living: vulnerability and safeguarding

Introduction

So far this book has promoted independent living, choice and control for disabled people. However there have been concerns expressed by professionals and family carers that some disabled people are at risk of coming to harm if left unsupported to manage their own care packages. There may well be a cultural view that disabled people should be protected and cared for, and there are systems in place for this to happen, yet:

> The ways that disabled lives are not protected, safeguarded or sustained, and the lower priority frequently accorded to children and adults living with impairment, are and have always been hazardous for disabled children and adults wherever they live. (Clements and Reid, 2008: 8)

Writings about neglect of and physical and sexual abuse against people who live in institutions have largely referred to people with learning difficulties and older people. National statistics had not been collected until 2009 and the resulting report *Abuse of Vulnerable Adults in England* (NHS Information Centre, 2011c) shows reports of abuse that are known by Local Authorities. The report uses the following definition for abuse:

> Abuse is a violation of an individual's human and civil rights by any other person or persons. Abuse may consist of a single act or repeated acts. It may be physical, verbal or psychological, it may be an act of neglect or an omission to act, or it may occur when a vulnerable person is persuaded to enter into a financial or sexual transaction to which he or she has not consented, or cannot consent. Abuse can occur in any relationship and may result in significant harm to, or exploitation of, the person subjected to it. (NHS Information Centre, 2011c: 35)

Statistics cannot be taken to be absolute facts, but rather they provide an indication of what is happening. This document is useful in giving such indications, it shows that 50 per cent of reports of abuse are against people with physical or sensory impairments, 21 per cent against people with learning difficulties, by age the largest group is 18–64-years-old (39 per cent), while the next largest group were aged 85 and over (25 per cent). More women were referred than men and the proportion increased with age, and there does not seem to be a statistical difference between ethnic groups (reported cases show a close match to population numbers at 11 per cent). People with physical impairments are the least likely of the client groups in the age range 18–64 to report sexual abuse, but most likely to be referred as neglected, abused physically, emotionally and financially. People aged 18–64 years have the highest reported incidents of alleged abuse in a public space.

Following the passing of the Convention on the Rights of Persons with Disabilities (CRPD), the United Nations Special Rapporteur of the Human Rights Council paid particular attention to the torture and other cruel, inhuman or degrading treatment or punishment of disabled people:

> 39. In the private sphere, persons with disabilities are especially vulnerable to violence and abuse, including sexual abuse, inside the home, at the hands of family members, caregivers, health professionals and members of the community.
>
> 40. Persons with disabilities are exposed to medical experimentation and intrusive and irreversible medical treatments without their consent (e.g., sterilization, abortion and interventions aiming to correct or alleviate a disability, such as electroshock treatment and mind-altering drugs including neuroleptics).
>
> 50. Torture, as the most serious violation of the human right to personal integrity and dignity, presupposes a situation of powerlessness, whereby the victim is under the total control of another person. Persons with disabilities often find themselves in such situations, for instance when they are deprived of their liberty in prisons or other places, or when they are under the control of their caregivers or legal guardians. In a given context, the particular disability of an individual may render him or her more likely to be in a dependant situation and make him or her an easier target of abuse. However, it is often circumstances external to the individual that render them 'powerless', such as when one's exercise of decision-making and legal capacity is taken away by discriminatory laws or practices and given to others. (Nowak, 2008: 9)

This chapter will consider the issues of harm to disabled people. Before considering the specifics of risk and safeguarding within adult social care, consideration is given to what it is that disabled people may be vulnerable to in a wider context, and where the need to be safeguarded comes from. Some of these potential threats are blatant and others are insidious, such as the way in which media representations indicate that there is a widespread perception that disabled people are a drain on society, and that there is too much expense in providing health and personal care. There is also a eugenic view that disabled people are a threat to the gene pool of the human species, which links in with certain aspects of racism. These negative views can contribute to contempt and hostility toward disabled people which may not be immediately recognised as safeguarding issues, yet they are all part of the milieu that can put disabled people into vulnerable situations.

Lessons from the past and meaning for today

Eugenics and euthanasia

The value of the lives of people with impairments has long been under question. This is starkly illustrated by events in the middle of the twentieth century, especially but not exclusively by the Third Reich of Nazi Germany. Eugenics is a philosophy and practice of keeping the human species 'pure' by encouraging the most able and strongest to procreate, while preventing those considered likely to degenerate the species. Compulsory sterilisation was used in several countries in the mid twentieth century as this was seen as a means to prevent such degeneration (Friedlander, 1995). Euthanasia had originally meant a patient could ask a doctor to help them to die more quickly and less painfully than would be if left to let nature take its course. However the meaning and practice of euthanasia changed to fit in with eugenic ideals. This change meant that others could judge that the patient was suffering, relatives and doctors were allowed to make the decision to end a disabled person's life in order to alleviate suffering. Disabled people were also being perceived as unproductive and an economic burden, the criteria for those disabled people who would be included in the mass killings were based on their perceived ability to work:

> It was pointed out that, during the war, in numerous cases, healthy people had to give up their lives and these severely ill people continued to live and would continue to live unless this action started, and that, in addition, the nursing situation and

the nourishment situation would justify the elimination of these people. (Friedlander, 1995:82)

During this period disabled people became known as 'useless eaters'.

Eugenics and euthanasia were not just issues in Germany, many disabled people were segregated in institutions, men and women were kept separate and many compulsorily sterilised in America and Europe before the Nazis took control in Germany (Lifton, 2000). In the United States for example, professionals, including social workers, were very much on board with the eugenic ideals in relation to developing social planning (Friedlander, 1995). In the United Kingdom Richard Titmuss who was instrumental in starting social work education at the LSE was also a prominent member of the Eugenics Society, which in the 1930s gave him access to an intellectual elite. However:

> It has been argued he was on the liberal wing of the movement and played a pivotal role in the attempt to get the Society to move away from the old behavioural and hereditarian arguments, and to encourage its members to emphasise the eugenic significance of nutrition and other environmental factors. (Welshman, 2004: 228)

In Nazi Germany, the assessments which were carried out prior to deciding that a person was to be removed from their home and sent to an institution where they could be sterilised or killed bore a remarkable similarity to some aspects of social circumstance assessments carried out by social workers (see Burleigh, 2000).

The dehumanisation of disabled people by the Nazis in Germany did not originate with them, they used it to their own ends and the European and American milieu just made it easier for the Nazis to implement their programme. It was not such a huge step to the first phase of the holocaust – was the killing of thousands of disabled people in the Aktion-T4 programme. Lifton (2000) was struck by the ordinary lives of the medical professionals, yet they became central to the Nazi holocaust, they carried out the most evil of actions segregating it from other areas of their lives. The killings were portrayed as mercy killings of people who were suffering due to the medical conditions or impairments they had:

> Dr Karl Brandt, one of the main perpetrators of Aktion-T4, was found guilty of crimes against humanity and executed along

with six others, although he maintained to the last that the programme was an act of mercy. He said, 'I am fully conscious that when I said "Yes" to euthanasia I did so with the deepest conviction, just as it is my conviction today, that it was right.' (Crow, 2010: 24)

The Nazis perfected their techniques on disabled people before moving on to murder Jews and others:

At least 70,000 disabled people were killed during the official Aktion-T4 programme but this was also followed by an unofficial period of 'wild euthanasia' in which individual medics carried out their own killings in institutions throughout Germany using starvation, poisoning, shooting and electric shock treatments. The final death toll is estimated at 250,000 but this number could well be higher, since many disabled people who were slaughtered in concentration camps do not appear in these statistics. (Crow, 2010: 23)

The killings continued in other institutions after the Aktion-T4 programme ended (Mostert, 2002). The courts were not entirely unsympathetic to those who allowed the killings to continue and few were prosecuted (Crow, 2010).

While not at the extreme end of the continuum all of this background resonates in the cultural and societal value afforded to disabled people today in the United Kingdom and other parts of the world. At the time of writing there are changes to the welfare state which are intended to save costs by reducing numbers of people claiming disability benefits. There are concerns about the way in which disabled people are being portrayed as a burden and contribute to the cultural negative perception of disabled people bears similarities to the early twentieth century:

Disabled People are being painted as a drain on society, an expensive burden we can no longer afford. This is not only insulting it also fails to recognise the invaluable contribution that Disabled People make in society. Through paid work, voluntary work, community involvement. One in four people in society have some type of impairment. Do we really believe that society would be better off without all those people. Brings back disturbing memories from history doesn't it? (Southampton CIL, 2010)

Finkelstein and Stuart (1996) argue that threats to the lives of people with impairments begin in the womb. They called for the end to pregnancy screening programmes, pointing out that the impairment of a foetus places no additional risk on the mother during pregnancy or at birth and that the future quality of life of the child is not a ground for abortion. They highlight instead the need for family support and the right of the child not to be over-protected on some false assumption of their inability to take responsibility for themselves, as well as the ending of segregated education.

The continued ill treatment and other forms of discrimination that disabled people endure indicate that the contempt and hostility toward disabled people is simply a matter of degree.

Assisted dying

While suicide is legal in the United Kingdom, attempts to take one's own life are usually taken very seriously and much effort is made to prevent people from doing so, although this may not always extend to disabled people. The reasons that people may commit or attempt suicide are varied and most people who succeed do this without the involvement or prior knowledge of another person. The 1961 Suicide Act makes it an offence to encourage or assist a suicide or a suicide attempt in England and Wales. Anyone doing so could face up to 14 years in prison. However, in recent years there has been considerable media and public interest in people with serious medical conditions who feel that their lives are not worth living and much empathy for those who assist them to die. These discussions and debates have tended to make negative assumptions about the value of life when someone is chronically ill or disabled, and about the factors that cause people to become suicidal.

While there is some recognition that the wish to die may be influenced by poor health and social care, the link with people with physical impairments or life threatening conditions and whether they have appropriate support is not always made. One organisation that has been associated with this issue is *Dignity in Dying*, which claims to support changes in the law to allow assisted dying for people who are terminally ill rather than for chronically ill or disabled people, and to promote improvements in social and personal care (www.dignityindying.org.uk). However *Dignity in Dying* are better known for their connections with cases such as that of Debbie Purdey who went to court to seek assurance that if she asks her partner to provide the means for her death, that he would not be prosecuted. This position has gained support in several quarters, but the law remains unchanged, that is it remains illegal to assist another person in their suicide.

Media reports indicate that there is confusion between people who are close to death and those who have physical impairments. When a disabled person whose condition is not life threatening says they want the facility of an assisted death, questions are not always asked about how a lack of support may lead to the option of death seeming better than life. That the person concerned wants to die can be viewed as a matter of common sense:

> It was a breakthrough this week when the director of public prosecutions decided not to bring charges against Daniel James's parents for helping their son kill himself at Dignitas in Switzerland. The young man paralysed in a rugby accident had his wishes respected by his reluctant parents. To be physically incapacitated should not take away the right everyone else has to take their own life if they choose. (Toynbee, 2008)

Even though Daniel James did not have a terminal disease the Director of Public Prosecutions (DPP) decided it was not in the public interest to prosecute his parents who facilitated his death. Of course acquiring a major impairment is extremely traumatic and drastic changes to lifestyle are inevitable. However, issues relating to disability from a social model perspective, such as exclusion, lack of support, isolation, lack of peer support and discrimination do not seem to be taken into account in deciding whether a life is worth living. The question has to be asked whether 23-year-old Daniel James spent any time with other young people with similar impairments many of whom have full and enjoyable lives, or whether he had control over his own personal assistants, had an accessible home, accessible transport, and how these things would make an enjoyable life a real possibility, while not having them could have made his life intolerable?

Toynbee (2008) also seems to assume that concerns about assisted suicide are for religious reasons adding 'Can the law be safely ignored now? No, it is only the beginning of the end of a religiously inspired edict that is as cruel as it is impractical' (Toynbee, 2008). This approach pays no heed to the concerns raised by those disabled people who support *Not Dead Yet UK*, which is a non-faith based network of people opposed to a change in the law. These disabled people express concerns that while struggling to get the support they need they have to justify their requirements, and many will feel obliged to bring their lives to an end in order to not be a burden. Disabled people who are involved with *Not Dead Yet UK* are acutely aware of the history of euthanasia and are extremely anxious about any proposed change to the law.

Baroness Campbell of Surbiton, Jane Campbell, is the founder of *Not Dead Yet* UK. Having been in a situation where she was ill in hospital and doctors assumed she would not want to be resuscitated, she not only had to get legal protection to ensure attempts to resuscitate her would be made, she had to remain awake for 48 hours in order to ensure she was not killed (Campbell, 2003). Sometime later she wrote:

> Sadly society still sees disabled people as tragic victims of their condition or diagnosis. And in my case without dignity because I need all physical tasks done for me. It is not unusual for me to hear 'I would rather be dead than live like that.' Views such as these are just as likely to be held by the medical profession as anyone else. After all they are just people drawn from a cross-section of society, subject to the same influences and negative stereotyping around disability as anyone else.
>
> It takes incredible strength to rise above these stereotypes and not to perceive them as fact. Some of us are fortunate enough to be able to challenge these assumptions. But stop and think: what if I couldn't speak up for myself, if I had no partner or carer that night to fight for my right to live? (Campbell, 2010:13)

Alison Davies is also part of the *Not Dead Yet UK* network; for ten years she wanted to die and made several attempts at suicide, until she discovered that there are things worth living for:

> Sometimes it's said that those who request death are just exercising their 'right to choose'. The problem is that often they feel they really 'have no choice' because support mechanisms are not in place. And of course they are not just 'choosing' for themselves. To say that death is in the best interests of some suffering people is to make value judgements about all who are disabled or terminally ill, and to suggest that death is a legitimate way of dealing with suffering. We can do better for suffering people than killing them, but legalising medical killing would militate against the further development of social and palliative care services to help us to live.

Once it is established that it is acceptable to cause death as a way of 'preventing suffering' no sick or disabled person will be safe. (Not Dead Yet UK, 2011: online)

Social workers may encounter disabled people who are considering asking for assistance to die and they need to ensure that disabled people have the support they need to lead a full life. They need to remember that when the case is made about supported dying this often focuses on the medical conditions only and issues such as discrimination and lack of support to lead a full life are completely ignored. Peer support is crucial and again the role of Centres for Independent Living is valuable.

Social workers also need to be clear that:

A person commits an offence under section 2 of the Suicide Act 1961 if he or she does an act capable of encouraging or assisting the suicide or attempted suicide of another person, and that act was intended to encourage or assist suicide or an attempt at suicide. (Crown Prosecution Service 2010)

In particular social workers need to be aware that a prosecution is more likely to be required if:

(14) the suspect was acting in his or her capacity as a medical doctor, nurse, other healthcare professional, a professional carer (whether for payment or not), or as a person in authority, such as a prison officer, and the victim was in his or her care; (Crown Prosecution Service, 2010)

Although there may not be specific guidance for social workers, the British Medical Association (2010: 2) guidance for responding to patient requests may also be used by social workers:

The BMA advises doctors to avoid all actions that might be interpreted as assisting, facilitating or encouraging a suicide attempt. This means that doctors should not:

- advise patients on what constitutes a fatal dose;
- advise patients on anti-emetics in relation to a planned overdose;
- suggest the option of suicide abroad;
- write medical reports specifically to facilitate assisted suicide abroad; nor
- facilitate any other aspects of planning a suicide.

Institutional abuse

As discussed in earlier chapters residential accommodation is too often the only choice available to disabled people, society may consider this to be a place of safety but this is not necessarily so. Despite subsequent amendment of the *National Assistance Act 1948*, in particular by the *NHS and Community Care Act 1990*, the statutory duty to provide residential accommodation remains though it must now be achieved through purchasing the majority of such services from the private and voluntary sectors. The 1948 Act recognised a powerful historical tradition for charitable agencies to be involved in such provision and thereby permitted local authorities to delegate their powers to approved agencies if they so wished. Some authorities chose to do this, and the largest agency providing residential accommodation for disabled people was Cheshire Homes, now Leonard Cheshire Disability with a network of almost 100 homes throughout the United Kingdom. More recently the private sector has been developing.

Looking back once again to the 1970s and the view of institutions from the perspective of a member of UPIAS, many of whom lived in such institutions:

> The cruelty, petty humiliation, and physical and mental deprivation suffered in residential institutions, where isolation and segregation have been carried to extremes, lays bare the essentially oppressive relations of this society with its physically impaired members. As in most similar places, such as special schools, there are some staff and volunteers doing their best to help the residents. But their efforts are systematically overwhelmed by the basic function of segregated institutions, which is to look after batches of disabled people – and in the process convince them that they cannot realistically expect to participate fully in society and earn a good living. (UPIAS, 1975: 3)

Some of those involved with UPIAS who lived in a Cheshire Home asked for research into the lives of disabled people confined to residential institutions. This research was conducted by Miller and Gwynne and published in 1971. They reported that:

> by the very fact of committing people to institutions of this type, society is defining them as, in effect, socially dead then the essential task to be carried out is to help the inmates to make their

transition from social death to physical death. (Miller and Gwynne, 1972: 89)

In the twenty-first century many disabled people fear that they will not receive the support they require and could end up 'in a home', losing autonomy and privacy. Living in an institution, or attending a day centre are all fairly automatic ways of entrenching unemployability and instilling fear in many disabled people. The institution (a home) takes control of the lives of inmates – more recently termed 'residents', movement is restricted, choice over meal times and bedtimes are withdrawn (more so in some than in others), choice over who you wish to spend time with – or just as importantly *not* spend time with is often lost. Practices in institutions can desensitise all those involved to the more subtle ways in which personal liberty is restricted and how this is inevitably abusive – no longer noticing the individual who is kept waiting after asking for a drink or to be assisted to the toilet, who is left sitting in a state of monotony for hours on end without any kind of stimulation, or left sitting next to someone they do not like, denied the opportunity to go out, to socialise and meet new people:

> Powerlessness characterises the experience of residential care and the nature of institutionalisation affects even those of us who are not in residential care. The possibility of institutionalisation hangs over many disabled people living in our own homes, fuelled by the fear that one day the support which makes our independence possible will disappear, or that an increase in functional limitation will prove too much for whatever resources are available to us. (Morris, 1991: 127)

The misery of life in an institution has international recognition and the United Nations Special Rapporteur of the Human Rights Council expresses concern over the way in which usual practice in institutions is ill treatment, but not recognised as such:

> The Special Rapporteur draws the attention of the General Assembly to the situation of persons with disabilities, who are frequently subjected to neglect, severe forms of restraint and seclusion, as well as physical, mental and sexual violence. He is concerned that such practices, perpetrated in public institutions, as well as in the private sphere, remain invisible and are not recognized as torture or other cruel, inhuman or degrading treatment or punishment. (Nowak 2008:2)

However, at the time of writing there are Government proposals to remove the mobility component of the Disability Living Allowance (or its replacement Personal Independence Payment) for people living in institutions, this can only add to their misery.

Getting out of segregated provision once in there is also extremely difficult, if not impossible. Having been to a special school and then into a Leonard Cheshire home Anna McNaughton in her early twenties, is trapped. The home where she lives and has established networks is not in the area of the Local Authority that is funding her, if she moves into her own home in the same area her funding authority will stop funding her, while the new authority refuses to give any funding as they argue this is not her ordinary residence. Anna has considerable physical impairments and she stated, 'If I could move into my own place I'd feel more independent to make more decisions about what's best for me. I'd feel really proud of myself' (Salman, 2010).

Blunden and Ash, (2007) claim that the guidance is so vague that there are hundreds of disabled people in this situation, large sums of money are spent on keeping people in institutions where they do not want to be:

> Large sums of money are wasted in administrative and legal costs in seeking to resolve such disputes and in some cases people are prevented from moving into cheaper forms of care or independent life-styles. These disputes cause untold distress and the waste of millions of pounds of public money. Yet solving these problems need not cost the taxpayer a penny; indeed money could well be saved. This is unthinking discrimination against disabled people by various elements of state bureaucracy and is an infringement of their human rights. (Blunden and Ash, 2007: 6)

So even before considering any examples of individual abuse the very nature of residential institutions, despite improvements over the years, is oppressive. Being trapped in an institution and effectively being denied a private and family life is a form of abuse by the state. Just as children are made vulnerable to abuse by being placed in institutions, disabled adults have also become victims of assaults and of other acts of hostility that are not deemed illegal by society.

> The recent entry into force of the Convention on the Rights of Persons with Disabilities ... provides a timely opportunity to

review the anti-torture framework in relation to persons with disabilities. By reframing violence and abuse perpetrated against persons with disabilities as torture or a form of ill-treatment, victims and advocates can be afforded stronger legal protection and redress for violations of human rights. (Nowak 2008:2)

As already indicated statistical information about abuse of disabled people is sparse, but the data gathered from referrals of abuse (NHS Information Centre, 2011c) indicates that 32 per cent of alleged abuse takes place in a residential or care home, which compares to 38 per cent being in a person's own home. Also in 24 per cent of referrals, the allegation was against a social-care worker. The likelihood of being abused by another 'vulnerable person' appears to be highest for people with a physical impairment (NHS Information Centre, 2011c: 9). There are about 230,000 people living in a care or nursing home (NHS Information Centre, 2010) and given that most disabled people live in their own home it seems that the likelihood of abuse in an institution is much higher, also the likelihood of contact with another 'vulnerable' adult is higher in social care settings than a domestic setting. This has to raise questions about whether disabled people are any safer in a care setting than managing their own care.

Hate crime

The term 'hate crime' is best known in relation to 'race', faith and homophobic attacks, more recently it has been used in relation to targeted attacks against disabled people. The definition used by the Crown Prosecution Service is:

Any incident which is perceived to be based upon prejudice towards or hatred of the victim because of their disability or so perceived by the victim or any other person. (Crown Prosecution Service, 2006: 10)

Although the number of recorded attacks is much lower in relation to disabled people than for other groups, this does not mean there are fewer attacks, but there could be a lack of recognition that these attacks, even when reported, should be recorded or thought of as hate crimes. A complication is the notion that disabled people are 'vulnerable'; an attack which is thought to be motivated by the perception of vulnerability is considered a lesser offence than where hatred was the motivation for an attack:

> However not all crimes against disabled people are disability hate crimes. Some crimes are committed because the offender regards the disabled person as being vulnerable and not because the offender dislikes or hates disabled people. (Crown Prosecution Service, 2006: 9)

Roulstone *et al.* (2011: 356–7) comment:

> It is perhaps odd that having established the powers that attach to hate disablist crime responses, that blanket exceptions come into play where crimes are seen to be motivated not by hatred but by perceived 'vulnerability' of a disabled person. Whilst safeguards are clearly required, it is concerning that vulnerability should weaken disabled people's rights to legal redress ... Unless we take the view that vulnerability, pity, tragedy are all benign assumptions about disability which are very different to discrimination, prejudice, hostility and hate then we begin to question the edifice on which disablist 'hate crime' policy and law are built.

There has been little formal research into disablist hate crime, however, a study of organisational responses and perceptions of disablist 'hate crime' in the North West of England (Roulstone and Thomas, 2009) was able to provide a good picture of the challenges of responding to disablist hate crime. The authors noted that the response rate of 10 per cent was disappointing but commented that this is probably a sign of the poor infrastructure for the reporting of hate crime in many places and that many workers in third party reporting centres did not recognise disability hate crime. Reluctance to report hate crime may also be because asking 'disabled people to define themselves individually as objects of hatred in the eyes of the law demands a great deal in a culture which is often unthinkingly disabling' (Piggott, 2011: 32).

Given that there is a paucity of research indicating the numbers of attacks against disabled people Thomas (2011) used information from a dossier on Disability Now's website about disability 'hate crimes'. This gave brief descriptions of 51 incidents of hostility against disabled people, the majority of whom (31) were people were with physical impairments followed by 13 people with learning difficulties (Disability Now, 2010: online). The addition of two incidents reported in the press both of whom died following targeted attacks, gave evidence of 53 incidents (one incident involved two people):

> Only two of the incidents were treated as 'hate crime' by police, in 10 cases people were described as vulnerable. Thirteen incidents involved the death of the individual, 5 of these were murders, and one manslaughter. There were 27 incidents of theft and 23 of assault. Fourteen attacks were noted to have followed earlier repeated attacks. Ten people were tipped out of their wheelchair or scooter. Nine perpetrators were 'friends' or relatives, they were most likely to be involved with people with learning difficulties. It seems people with learning difficulties were most likely to die, be robbed, and held captive, whilst wheelchairs users are likely to be tipped out of their wheelchairs and robbed. (Thomas, 2011: 108)

There is not enough known about the motivation for disablist hate crime, but as pointed out earlier the perspective that disabled people have lives not worthy of life is likely to play a role (Gallagher, 1990; Clements and Read, 2003). Crow (2010) draws links between the eugenics and euthanasia of the mid twentieth century to current issues:

> In a time of rising hate crime against disabled people and a society that still holds numerous physical barriers and prejudices, it can seem overwhelming. Increased pre-natal screening and the abortion of foetuses with impairments, and hurried measures to legalise assisted suicide raise questions about the value of disabled people's lives and even their right to exist. (Crow, 2010: 24)

Government statistics (NHS Information Centre, 2011c) show that around 90 per cent of cases of abuse were reported by professionals, while referrals from a family member, friend of neighbour or self-referral amount to only around 10 per cent. So for those people who are not known to social services, the likelihood of them self-referring seems to be very low indeed.

The term 'hate crime' can cover a variety of hostile incidents; attacks against disabled people can be perpetrated by strangers or acquaintances – with similarities to racist or homophobic violence. However disabled people can be subjected to hostility from people with whom they have very close relationships. Thomas (2011: 108) distinguishes between hate crime and mate crime.

'Hate crime' – violent attacks which are perpetrated by 'outsiders', not a part of the disabled person's household, or outsiders may enter the home purely to carry out the attack. There is little or no relationship between the perpetrators and the disabled person, they may be recognised as living in the area, but there is no reciprocal arrangement or inter-dependency. The disabled person does not welcome any part of any relationship there may be. These may be opportunistic attacks, or may be long term repeated, sustained attacks.

'Mate crime' – the hostile acts of perpetrators who are 'insiders', sharing domesticity to some degree, there is a mutual relationship. The disabled person may cling to the relationship, wanting the hostility to stop but welcoming the company and feeling part of a family or group. These situations are not opportunistic, they are calculated. Disabled people in these situations are less likely to complain to the police or other authorities because they consider the perpetrators to be their friends, they may justify the violence.

It will sometimes be clear that disabled people are living with people or have been 'befriended' by people who are abusing them, yet hostilities can go barely recognised, they can occur in situations where social workers may consider a disabled person is well cared for. There can easily be a situation that allows carers and pseudo-friends, if they are so minded, to take control of:

- where the disabled person lives;
- who they live with;
- when they get in or out of bed;
- when they may use the toilet;
- what they wear;
- if they get out of the house;
- who they are friends with, and when or if they have contact; and/or
- what and when they eat.

They can control behaviour or punish by:

- knowingly leaving equipment and other items out of reach;
- knowing making the home inaccessible;
- withholding personal care; and
- withhold medication.

They can take advantage of a situation for personal gain, including:

- make fraudulent use of blue car parking badges;
- making the Motability car their own, while the disabled person does not get to use it; and/or
- claiming carer's allowance, but not actually supporting the disabled person.

These activities are not usually considered to be crimes and can easily be carried out without argument let alone violence. However, they are all ways for one individual to achieve power over another. These acts are carried out by ordinary people, in ordinary homes and would probably not be considered to be unreasonable behaviour by those carrying them out, the disabled person themselves, or others (Thomas, 2011).

Social workers need to be alert to identifying and safeguarding against disablist 'hate crime', but it is not straightforward. Even where there is obvious hostility having it identified as such is complicated, the circumstances in which disabled people find themselves in order to receive the support they need, or in order to have relationships can lead to them live in hostile and abusive situations.

Abuse of disabled children

Despite the issue of abuse being a major concern in relation to non-disabled children, disabled children have remained largely hidden with respect to child protection until quite recently. In the past decade the particular vulnerability of disabled children to abuse has been (a) an issue for Safeguarding Services (Chief Inspectors, 2005), (b) specified in the safeguarding procedures of many social services authorities, (c) the subject of concern at the Council of Europe (Brown, 2003), and (d) included within mainstream child protection textbooks such as the chapter by Kitson and Clawson (2007) in the third edition of *The Child Protection Handbook*.

Several writers (Brown and Craft, 1989; Kennedy, 1989; Kelly, 1992; Marchant and Page, 1992; Middleton, 1992; 1995, 1999; Westcott, 1993; Westcott and Cross, 1995; Morris, 1997b, 1998, 2002; Read and Clements, 2001) had discussed the issue prior to this and had identified that disabled children not only are more likely to be abused and are more likely to live away from home, but that there are also some additional forms of abuse that may be specific to them:

Disabled children living away from home are particularly vulnerable. In addition to the risk factors that exist for all children in residential settings, disabled children are at risk of particular forms of abuse. These include overmedication, poor feeding and toileting arrangements, issues around control of challenging behaviour, lack of stimulation, information and emotional support. (NSPCC, 2003: 23).

There are three main issues that are particularly significant to child protection in relation to disabled children, first, child protection services have ignored the abuse because they have failed to acknowledge that it could happen, or because services that are geared to families have missed the abuse that occurs in residential school settings, or because abusive acts towards disabled children have been treated as a normal and tolerable reaction of over-stressed parents, or because social workers lack the appropriate communication skills.

Second, the institutionalisation of disabled children by the education system in particular leaves them not only vulnerable to abuse by non-family members it also denies them a role in mainstream society that other children enjoy. Furthermore there is bullying within schools whether mainstream or segregated (Chief Inspectors, 2008: 31).

Finally, the imposition of non-disabled normality through activities such as conductive education, and the psycho-emotional effects of disablism can act as a form of identity abuse (Reeve, 2002). While there may now be better recognition of the abuse of disabled children within safeguarding agencies, the long-standing hegemony of the individual model of disability may mean that social workers still fail to treat disabled children as worthy of their attention as non-disabled children. Middleton (1995: 70) argued that child protection research tends to conceptualise child abuse as socially constructed, reflecting the values of society. If this is essentially true, it follows that the official failure to deal with the abuse of disabled children reflects a cultural lack of concern for their welfare. Disabled children will only be better protected when we learn as a society to value them equally.

The purpose of this section is to highlight the most pertinent issues that affect disabled children and to consider what the social model might mean in terms of the response of social work, the police and courts which have tended to see such abuse as unbelievable or the fantasy of disabled children.

Morris (1997b), in a review of literature on the placement of disabled children in boarding schools and care homes, found that social services departments may be using such placements as a means of avoiding intervening in childcare issues and this may have included cases of abuse to disabled children. This not only reflects discrimination against individual children, but on an institutional level it is qualitatively different to the response to non-disabled children. Middleton (1995) argued that social workers must respond to the challenge of child abuse as part of an anti-oppressive practice that leads to a breakdown of artificial institutional boundaries which does not seek to polarise the interests of the child and the parents, on the basis of one being the victim of the other who is totally bad. However, child protection services are, as always, facing their own political and practice problems that often militate against the inclusion of disability issues.

The final issue here is concerned with emotional abuse and the denial of self-identity. The development of a positive self-identity is necessary to individuals seeking to assert their own value and citizenship alongside others. The practice of conductive education has already been referred to and has long been the subject of debate (Beardshaw, 1993; Oliver, 1993), nevertheless it serves as a good example of what emotional abuse might mean in relation to disabled children's identity.

What is problematic about conductive education is that its purpose is to train people to conform to a non-disabled definition of normality, the regime is gruelling, leaving little time or energy for pleasure in life for the child or family, and in the process devalues diversity. Similarly when Deaf children have been prevented from learning sign language by being sent to special schools that only allow lip reading they have been denied the right to become part of a linguistic culture and are expected to conform to the hearing norm. Morris (1992: 6) described the importance of pride to disabled people:

> When a mother says that she loves her child 'in spite' of that child's disability, she is saying that she does not love the disabled part of her child. When the Spastics Society urges the public to 'see the person and not the wheelchair', they are being asked to ignore something that is central to our experience. And when our achievements are applauded as 'overcoming all odds', the disabled part of us is being denied and diminished.

Valuing us as people should not mean ignoring the things about our bodies which make us different. In asserting our rights we also want to take pride in ourselves. We cannot do this unless this pride incorporates the way we are different.

In a society that is dominated by the individual model in which normality is seen as the lack of any impairment, it is difficult for anyone who deviates from this norm to develop a positive self-identity, as they are treated as abnormal. Yet this has been identified as an important element of the struggle of disabled people to remove the barriers that confront them, this is quite different to overcoming difficulties in the functional sense. Childhood is a formative period of life and the impact both then and later in adulthood of having one's life devalued can be enormous. Emotional abuse is not usually considered as important as the other forms of abuse – physical, sexual and neglect – but the potential for it to occur within a society that devalues impairment is high (Reeve, 2004) so it is a matter that should underpin social work with disabled children, both within child protection and elsewhere.

Risk

Social workers need to be alert to the risk of abuse that comes from others. Often those who work in the protection services find it difficult to believe that adults and children they see only as vulnerable could ever be the target of an abuser, despite the evidence that abusers take advantage of vulnerability. This reflects the social norm of viewing disability as a personal tragedy and seeing disabled people only in terms of the help and assistance they need, rather than as having the same potential for risk as non-disabled people, particularly when that potential may be greater.

Another source of risk comes from the dominant ideology that sees disabled people as a burden on an otherwise happy family, maybe forgiving lapses of impatience in parents and carers. So social workers, as representatives of the welfare system, may consider that much of the abuse that disabled people suffer is acceptable. While this certainly arises from the failure to see disabled people as anything more than dependent and as the cause of the problem, it also reflects some collusion on the part of social workers and their agencies, by their failure to provide adequate support to disabled people and their families.

A further risk is that some abuse may not be recognised as such, for example, rough handling of adults or children requiring personal assistance, or the failure to ensure that certain aids and equipment are fitted properly, or are changed as a child grows. This is reframed in terms of the treatment of the disabled person rather than as a form of abuse, reflecting the individual model's medicalisation of disablement.

In some cases problem arise because the child or adult safeguarding services have no means of communicating with many disabled people. This is both in terms of the lack of communication skills such as sign language, but also due to the tendency to understand the world, including abuse, in terms of a non-disabled culture. Throughout the welfare system and society at large, the issue of communication is seen as a problem of the individual who cannot talk or hear, rather than as society's failure to be inclusive of other communication systems. The result of this is that disabled people are often unable to give evidence or even be heard.

Finally, as previously mentioned, abuse may be considered as an acceptable price to pay for otherwise resolving an administratively difficult problem. Many children for example are sent to residential schools, or may be placed with foster families, or adults sent to residential homes in which they are subsequently abused. These resources may be quite scarce because of the reluctance of other foster parents or of mainstream schools to accommodate disabled children, so the additional problem to social services of finding a suitable placement for a child if the child was to be removed outweighs the abuse. While this may be the most advantageous option from an administrative perspective, it is not, in the language of childcare, in the best interests of the child. The lack of accessible housing and support at home for adults and children also leads to disabled people of all ages being placed in vulnerable situations.

These reactions to impairment in adults and children illustrate the depth of the influence of the individual model within social work. The institutional structures of social services agencies and the cultural beliefs of social workers both tend to militate against an approach that treats disabled people of all ages appropriately. The problem however is not simply one of an inadequate response, but also possibly one of collusion.

So far this chapter has painted a very negative picture of the abuse endured by disabled people, yet none of this emanates from disabled people themselves, it is society with its cultures and systems that cause it. This is where change needs to happen, and where safeguards need to be located. Instead restrictions tend to be put on disabled people to protect them from risk. Professional and family fears that the personalisation agenda is too risky for many disabled people leads them to place restrictions on disabled people and deny them choice, control and enjoyment in life. These problems are not resolved by simple policy changes, important as that is, what is also required is for the culture of understanding to be changed. This can only be achieved by challenging the assumptions on which it is based and which have been internalised by many social workers and agencies, or they will continue to curtail those who seek to practice appropriately.

Individual risk is an inevitable part of life and is usually balanced against the positives of an activity. For example, the risk of road accidents does not prevent people using private cars for the benefits they bring. Yet this balance is denied disabled people and the Disability Rights Commission (2006:1) noted that 'nothing appears to stand in the way of stamping out risk – not our liberty, cost, efficiency, the truth and not it seems, ridicule' and, 'If disabled people are to become equal citizens, then the damage being done in all areas of life by the issue of 'risk' must be challenged' (2006: 6).

Furthermore the Department of Health (2010a: 6) has noted that when people's lives are not under the control of others they are at less, rather than more risk:

> People who have choice and control over their support arrangements, keep in touch with family and friends, and stay active and healthy, are likely to be at less risk of abuse than those who are isolated and dependent on services. They are also more likely to have people in their lives that would notice and take action in response to any concerns of abuse.

Ensuring personalisation is carried out properly within the context of communities is a good way of safeguarding individuals. As discussed earlier there is a need for a cultural shift in social work in order to allow disabled people to have choice and control, this includes people being able to take risks:

> Risk-management is about working with a person using services in order to explore the levels of risk they want to take. It requires a cultural change for staff which includes a change in the way that risk is understood, managed and negotiated. Working in a truly person-centred way avoids the risks of

making assumptions. It encourages an approach that considers the particular circumstances of the individual and any problems that have gone before. In designing support arrangements that suit an individual, safety remains one of the goals. (Department of Health, 2010a: 8)

It should be assumed that disabled people can make a judgement about risk unless all attempts have been made to support them in making decisions and it is proven that they cannot so do. This is a requirement of the Mental Capacity Act 2005 and of Article 12 of the Convention on the Rights of Persons with Disabilities. 'State parties shall recognize that persons with disabilities enjoy legal capacity on an equal basis with others in all aspects of life.' (United Nations, online)

Where individuals do need support in deciding whether risk is proportionate and balanced this can be done jointly and the risk of losing independence must also be given priority. Even making small choices can make a huge difference to individuals, and they should not be over-ruled by someone who thinks they know better.

Social workers need to show that they have been reasonable in balancing risk and it is important to record how decisions have been made so that that there is a paper trail of evidence.

CHAPTER OVERVIEW

- There is a long history of abuse of disabled people – cultures and societal systems allow this to happen.
- Risk is a part of everyday life for everyone and certain safeguards are required against risks.
- Risk and safeguards have to be balanced against benefits that are connected with certain life choices.
- Safeguards need to focus on societal and cultural causes of abuse.
- Safeguards should not take away disabled people's potential to have the freedom to enjoy life and be part of their communities.
- Social workers need to work in partnership with disabled people to get the right balance, and they need to keep adequate records of how decisions have been arrived at.

Points for reflection

Exercise 1

Carry out a web search for media interest in 'mercy killing', this may be assisted suicide or family members who kill a disabled relative whether the disabled person asks to be killed or not. Make a note of your findings and consider whether the coverage is balanced. Is the voice of disabled people with physical impairments, who argue that the law should not be changed, adequately reflected?

Exercise 2

Observe media representations of disabled people for two weeks, this can cover newspapers, magazines, TV, radio, theatre, cinema and so on. Make a note of your findings and consider whether these are likely to promote respect or contempt for disabled people.

Further resources

Department of Health (2009) *Safeguarding Adults – Report on the Consultation on the Review of 'No secrets: guidance on developing and implementing multi-agency policies and procedures to protect vulnerable adults from abuse'*.
This describes how the consultation took place and analyses the responses, it does not include a government response.

Roulstone, A., Thomas, P. and Balderston, S. (2011) 'Between Hate and Vulnerability: Unpacking the British Criminal Justice System's Construction of Disablist Hate Crime', *Disability and Society*, 26(3): 351–64.
A paper about research into organisational response to disablist, homophobic and transphobic hate crime.

Roulstone, A. and Mason-Bish, H. (2012) *Disablist Hate Crime and Violence* (London: Routledge).

Scragg, T. and Mantell, A. (2011) *Safeguarding Adults in Social Work*, 2nd edn (Exeter: Learning Matters Ltd).
A practical resource with case studies and related exercises.

Thomas, P. (2011) ' "Mate Crime": Ridicule, Hostility and Targeted Attacks against Disabled People', *Disability and Society*, 26(1): 107–11.
  Identifies the different characteristics of 'hate crime' and 'mate crime'.

Association for Real Change advises people with learning difficulties on how to avoid being drawn into situations that could make them vulnerable: www.arcsafety.net/

Not Dead Yet UK is a network of people who do not want a change in the law around assisted suicide: www.notdeadyetuk.org/

Roaring girl Productions produce resistance drama, on the plinth and conversation about the history of Aktion T4, the Nazi programme of mass-murder targeting disabled people, on what it means today: www.roaring-girl.com/productions/resistance-conversations/

CHAPTER 7

Conclusion: future directions

This final chapter brings together some of the issues thrown up by applying the social model of disability to social work as an organised professional activity. First, there are some theoretical and professional issues, then some organisational aspects and finally some strategies for the future.

Theoretical and professional developments

As noted previously, there have been some significant changes in the design and avowed purpose of welfare since the late 1990s. The introduction of direct payments, the emphasis on independent living, autonomy and empowerment in policy documents from the Department of Health, and the appointment of Jane Campbell (now Baroness Jane Campbell), the former Director of the National Council for Independent Living as the first Chair of the Social Care Institute for Excellence all suggested that the Labour government was serious about following a social model analysis of disability. However, their implementation strategy did not follow through as strongly, and those with responsibility for the delivery of social care have resisted the changes that would make a real difference to the lives of disabled individuals. While many of these changes have continued to develop under the coalition government, their assault on disabled people as a cause of the country's economic problems has strengthened social workers' opposition to policies such as personalisation (Dunning, 2011).

The main professional problem in trying to develop an adequate conceptualisation of social work in this area has been that there were few, if any, models or frameworks adequate for the purpose. Historically, the British Association of Social Workers (BASW) and the Central Council for Education and Training in Social Work (CCETSW) made attempts to define the roles and tasks of social workers with disabled people and to recommend levels of training that were needed (CCETSW, 1974; 1989; BASW, 1982; Stevens,

1991). The Department of Health's social work education requirements put 'disability' firmly within an individual model by placing it alongside human growth and development (Department of Health, 2002). Later the General Social Care Council (GSCC) stated very clearly in its post-qualifying requirements that social workers were expected to work in partnership with disabled people from a social model perspective (GSCC, 2005).

More recently the GSCC (2008: 56–7), through its Equality Diversity Scheme, reiterated its commitment to the social model of disability, but this is not apparent in implementation. Furthermore, the GSCC functions are being transferred to the Health Professions Council (HPC) in 2012, in its Equality Scheme the HPC uses the Disability Discrimination Act definition of disability adding that a main cause of the exclusion of disabled people is down to individual attitudes. As the HPC, which is a body mainly concerned with medical issues, does not seem to be thinking beyond individuals to societal systems and structures that act as disabling barriers, this is unlikely to facilitate the social understanding of disability in social work.

As far back as its 1990 AGM, BASW unanimously passed a motion recognising that disability resulted from the social reactions to impairment. In the same year it produced a discussion document on the subject (BASW, 1990). In it they described the nature of disability as initially caused by impairment, but that the impact of this on individuals and families depends on severity, prognosis, origin, social barriers, age, social impac, changes in personal functioning, and changes in social functioning. It went on to describe the social work role in terms of a series of functional tasks including taking responsibility for 'whether the disabled person can appreciate danger and act accordingly', clearly viewing independent living as potentially at odds with a societal responsibility to protect 'vulnerable' individuals. This description was little more than a reiteration of what had been happening within an individual model of practice, leaving the recommendations clearly at the technical knowledge/actual task levels. BASW's policy documents continue to reflect an individual model understanding of the problem, with fairly consistent use of the term 'people with disabilities'.

The document *Building a Safe and Confident Future: One year on* recommends standards should be streamlined, which is of course welcome. It also has a framework of nine professional standards, including 'Rights, justice and economic wellbeing: Advance human rights, and promote social justice and economic well-being' (Department for Education, 2010b:14). Key social work and social care organisations were also recently brought together by the Association of Directors of Adult Social Services (ADASS) and the Department of Health to produce a statement of what social work is, and what it hopes to achieve for adults:

Key outcomes for people are:

- choice and control;
- dignity and respect;
- economic well-being;
- improved quality of life;
- health and emotional well-being;
- making a positive contribution; and
- freedom from discrimination and harassment.

(ADASS/ Department of Health, 2010: 3)

These attempts to recognise, at least in terms of official policy, that disability arises as a consequence of social forces are welcome, but there is little evidence that this will be carried through and may not necessarily include responding to the need to develop a practice that is informed by such theorising.

Most attempts to develop a professional basis for the practice of social work with disabled people have never grasped with the perennial problem of the relationship between theory and practice, and the individual and social models of disability are dependent upon that relationship, either overtly or covertly. Thus, it could be said that the individual model stems from the 'personal tragedy theory of disability', whereas the social model stems from 'the social problem theory of disability'. Many policy statements are not robust enough to maintain a social model analysis. In practice someone with a very severe impairment may only be mildly disabled, whereas someone with a minor impairment may be totally disabled by poverty, poor housing, the attitudes of employers, or hostile social treatment. A scarce resource like professional expertise should be allocated on the extent of disability, not on the extent of impairment.

An attempt to look at this problem in the context of social work generally was made by Lee (Bailey and Lee, 1982: 16), who distinguished between three levels:

Level 1: *Actual task*
Level 2: *Technical knowledge*
Level 3: *Theoretical knowledge*

While ideally, good social work practice should be based upon an integration of all three levels, in reality there is often a polarisation between 'academics' and 'practitioners', with each group seeing its sphere of activity as unrelated to the other. Lee, however, suggested that 'speculative theory with scant regard for practice (level 1) is of little utility, and practice insulated from theoretical questions (level 3) while perfectly permissible in car maintenance, is downright dangerous in social work' (Bailey and Lee, 1982: 17). Within social work there has been a strong relationship between levels 1 and 2, whereas the relationship between levels 2 and 3 has remained weaker. Understanding and use of the social model of disability requires a stronger place for theoretical knowledge.

There have been a number of reasons for the social model still not having a strong position. First, until the 1980s articulated theories about disability were few and far between, as were considerations of their relationship to technical knowledge. Second, it is extremely difficult to draw up a skills' manual for social workers. Finally, much work with disabled people has been atheoretical, either based covertly upon the individual model of disability, or simply orientated to the immediate practical task at hand. As Lee (Bailey and Lee, 1982: 41) argued this approach has problems because:

> theory must have regard for practice but it should not be 'tailored' for it. Practical contingencies must not be allowed to dictate the terms of theoretical speculation, for if they do a most anaemic form of theorising will result. Such theory, raised in a protected environment to fit necessity, is the stuff of car maintenance manuals; and people informed by such manuals might be able to perform reasonably efficiently, but then so could unreflexive automatons.

Current examples of the maintenance of the individual model of disability include the government's paper *A Vision for Adult Social Care – Capable Communities and Active Citizens*. While this indicates a commitment to citizenship, it has a reliance on voluntarism in communities rather than rights to a certain level of support or a commitment to remove disabling barriers. However, the document's view that there should be user-led organisations, supported by local councils, is promising. Another example is the Law Commission's review of adult social care legislation that recommends that the confusing array of social care legislation should be replaced by a single piece of legislation. However welcome the idea of simplification might be, there are consequences. The Commission recommend that the 'overarching purpose of adult social care is to promote or contribute to the well-being of the individual. In effect, individual well-being must be the basis for all decisions made and actions carried out under the statute' (Law Commission, 2011: 20–1).

However, they consider well-being to be at odds with supporting people to be active citizens because this 'does not appear to be sufficiently precise to be capable of operating in legislation. There are also potential tensions between the two that would sit unhappily with the core idea of a single overarching principle' (Law Commission, 2011: 19).

These recommendations fall well short of tackling the societal causes of disability, indeed they are very likely to move social work further away from doing so. While the social model of disability would provide an adequate and appropriate base for developing social work practice with disabled people, much social work has been and is likely to remain inherently conservative and will not challenge existing social relations. Deeply embedded as it is in culture and social consciousness generally, the individual model, or personal disaster theory of disability can only be replaced or superseded by a radical change in both theoretical conceptualisation and practical approach. This has fundamental implications both for the training needs of social workers and for the professional organisation of social work. It was, and is not, enough merely to increase knowledge about disability on basic training courses; this must be tackled alongside a reversion towards specialist practice and away from the generic approach. Increasing diversity in the social work profession to ensure disabled people are included and an approach to widening participation in the new degree in social work is required as proposed by Sapey *et al.* (2004) and endorsed by the GSCC. While this is in accordance with aspects of a citizenship approach, more needs to occur in terms of changing the relationships between service providers and service users for the social model to be truly integrated into social work practice.

The paradox is that the BASW and the GSCC placed considerable importance on such values as empowerment, participation and choice in welfare and have taken a lead in this respect through the development of anti-oppressive practice in the social work curriculum. The foundation of such practice is that the social problems which individuals, families and communities face are often the result of systematic oppression within the structures of

British society. At the same time their adoption of a competence model of education has, according Froggett and Sapey (1997: 50) left social work:

> foundering in the mechanistic application of a political correctness which represents an ill-digested, prescriptive and rule-bound approach to which students must submit or rebel, but which they have little scope to interrogate and own, and the original point of which may well elude them.

A further contradiction, that suggests that the term 'anti-oppressive social work' is little more than an oxymoron, is the nature of social work values. Twenty years ago Holman (1993) argued that the ideology that underpinned the BASW's *Code of Ethics for Social Work* was in fact intensely individualistic:

> a focus which minimizes considerations of mutual obligations, of environment and structures, contains certain drawbacks. For a start it opens the door to explanations of human problems which stress the inadequacy of individuals regardless of their circumstances. This individualism has something in common with that of the New Right and its conception of an underclass of feckless individuals to be condemned and controlled. Then it diminishes the resolve to campaign against poverty and other societal forces, for they are regarded as outside the real scope of social work, which is just to deal with individuals. Not least, the climate that social work is to do with a professional coping with an individual client is a barrier to social workers acting collectively with user organizations and residents of communities. (Holman, 1993: 51–2)

However there are also two principles in the BASW's code of ethics that could be used in a social model way; to reduce disadvantage and exclusion, and to challenge the abuse of power. For Holman the solution lay in the development of mutuality as the basis of the relationship between the state, (and hence social workers as administrators of its welfare functions), and the recipients of welfare. Mutuality is a development of the socialist value of fraternity and a social work practice that is underpinned by this might be capable of responding to the criticisms of the social model analysis. Not only would it imply a mutual sharing of responsibility with disabled people and that the social work role was one of supporting individuals to achieve their own aspirations, it would also mean that for social workers to be truly effective in helping people to be less disabled, they would have to view the struggle of the disabled people's movement as directly affecting them also. The model of social work that would follow from this ideology would be based upon the notion that a world in which particular groups of people are systematically oppressed is oppressive to all people.

The individual model of disability and its associated themes of deviancy and abnormality are very much the product of the modernist project and the search for scientific certainty, yet still influenced by the traditional need for strong social hierarchies. In such a world people are identified, and develop a self-identity, as normal or abnormal, and the social model helps us to understand how this has become a systematic process of oppression. In the struggle against oppression, the oppressed will challenge the identity bestowed upon them, but what is also required is a similar challenge from the oppressors. Stuart Hall (quoted in Jaques, 1997: 34) argued that this was happening in relation to race:

> with globalisation comes the growing recognition that nobody has one identity. There isn't anyone who doesn't have complex cultural roots. The Brits suddenly discover half of them are really French, they speak a language partly based on Norse, they came from Scandinavia, they're Romans, many have gone to live in Australia and the Himalayas.

The result of this is to break down some of the notions that underpin racism and in particular the ideology of superiority that permits white people to justify their oppression of Black people. As discussed previously there are strong ideological links between racism and disablism. What is required in relation to disability is for non-disabled people to discover and accept that they may be as different from the ideal human body as those who they had considered as impaired, and as such are not part of a distinct and superior group.

To professionalise social work on the basis of an expertise in impairment as a cause of social need would be an act of oppression as this serves to reinforce theories of individual inadequacy and blame, whereas what is required is for social workers and social work to develop a commitment to the removal of disabling barriers in partnership with disabled people. This requires a fundamental shift towards a radical rather than an individualistic practice – the problems of disabled people, or social workers, are not resolved by the incorporation of empowerment as an instrumental competence within the curriculum. In part this is because of the anti-theoretical approach of competence-based education, but primarily it is because this actually represents part of the process of disempowering disabled people by providing bureaucratic measures to limit the effectiveness of protest and self-empowerment.

Organisational issues and structural developments

Three organisational concerns can be levelled at the services for disabled people.

1. Social workers act as arbiters of need between disabled people and the state.
2. The responsibilities for services for disabled people are uncoordinated and distributed between a large number of organisations and rehabilitation professions.
3. The services that are available tend to reflect the professional interests and aspirations of those workers rather than being based on any analysis of disability and the needs of disabled people.

The issue of the relationship between the needs of disabled people and the services provided is a complicated one in which there is no direct link between the two (see Figure 7.1). From this diagram it is clear that disabled people have their needs defined and interpreted by others, and the services provided to meet these needs are often delivered by large, bureaucratic organisations.

Social workers tend to be defensive about their role, often looking to their organisations as constraining their practice. However, the problem for social workers in social services departments is not merely one of a lack of opportunities to work in different ways, but is also exacerbated by the failure of the profession to distinguish between professional and administrative criteria for decision making, or to support workers who wished to make decisions based on the former rather than the latter. The administrative approach received official sanction through the *NHS and Community Care Act 1990* which, by introducing quasi-markets, also placed budget control at the top of local authority priorities.

Without challenging the basic principles of welfare that had been laid down in 1948, the changes that followed the Griffiths report were aimed at the structures of the relationship between government and the bureaucracy. Through the purchaser–provider split, its architects hoped to use market mechanisms, rather than

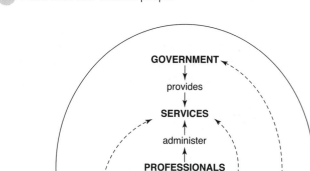

Figure 7.1 The relationship between needs and services
Source: M. Oliver, 1982: 57; reproduced with the permission of Michael Oliver.

professional judgement, as the major means for rationing services and keeping costs down. Community care plans of local authorities and strict controls over the size and use of budgets were the mechanisms through which this control would be directly exercised while the disciplines of the market would control the actions of individual practitioners and managers. We should question the extent to which this has been conducive to the development of a social work practice based on the social model of disability.

Some writers (for example Le Grand and Bartlett, 1993) have argued that these changes were necessary in order that the business of welfare could be conducted efficiently and equitably, but their analysis starts from traditional or individual model assumptions about the causes of social need. Others such as Holman are very clear that a system based upon the ideologies of the New Right has failed and will continue to do so:

> New Right policies have failed to revive the economy ... they have made a god out of Mamon so that personal gain and

material selfishness are regarded as virtues while the compassion for the disadvantaged and a readiness to share goods and power are sneered at as weaknesses. (Holman, 1993: 26)

This argument suggests that in order for the organisation of welfare to support the practice of social work within a social model analysis of disability, there would need to be a fundamental change to the ideologies that informed the structures of welfare.

The new Labour vision of welfare was as a mechanism to support people during periods of risk, that is, while they are temporarily unemployed. Rather than fundamentally changing the system, this built on the new right idea of individuals being responsible for their own welfare, but in need of support from time to time in order that more flexible employment markets can operate within the globalised capitalist economy. At a level of rhetoric the government then appeared keen to promote

disabled people's inclusion in the paid labour market with policies to revise the benefits system, and to make radical changes in the operation of the labour market. All these sound like social model solutions to the problem of high unemployment rate amongst disabled people. However, when the government talks about mechanisms to implement these changes, it focuses on two things: a small number of special schemes, and job coaches for individual disabled people. So while the government accepts that the problems are external to disabled people, its solutions target individual disabled people. (Oliver, 2004: 21)

Today the current government not only targets individual disabled people, they do so by withdrawing support rather than providing it.

Within social work it is the *Community Care (Direct Payments) Act, 1996* that is significant because, although it exploits the method of the market for the provision of care, it has the potential to shift the control and power over the purchase of services from local authorities to disabled people. Furthermore, with self-assessment of need, disabled people gain the opportunity to determine not only the best services but also their purpose. Within this structure there is potential for social workers to apply practice based on a social model understanding of disability, although the evidence tends to suggest considerable resistance to the direct payments system (CSCI, 2004) and personalisation (Dunning, 2011). The social work task should be one of supporting disabled people in the processes of assessing their own needs and purchasing their own personal assistance. Inevitably this affects the relationship between the helped and helper as personal assistants will be employees, not carers, and in the long term this has the potential to change the ways in which society views disabled people as dependent.

However, while the potential for change exists, it currently remains dependent upon the local authority's assessment of need and there are some barriers to this being conducted within a social model of disability. First, the tendency to require that disabled people have to come to terms with their impairment and disability before they can be successfully helped places a precondition on the assessment of need which reinforces normative assumptions about disability based upon an individual model. This problem was integral to the analysis that led CCETSW to assert that the self-assessment of need is essential to good social work practice (Stevens, 1991). Second, the continued emphasis on budgets limits the extent to which local authorities are prepared to relinquish their control in the determination of individual need; self-assessment requires a partnership between social workers and disabled people which threatens that control. The evidence in reviews of direct payment schemes shows that local authorities are quite creative in finding ways of resisting the changes the schemes were designed to achieve. Furthermore, social workers may be motivated to hold onto the assessment role in a non-participatory way as it is a significant source of power. While the Barclay report may have placed an emphasis on social care planning, community social work and counselling, for many social workers in local authorities their role has become one of social care administration, and a profession under threat may not be willing or able to assist others who are attempting to empower themselves.

Figure 7.1 is in itself simplistic and two additional aspects are important: first, the overlapping organisational context in which services are delivered; and second the people who deliver the services. Blaxter (1980) found that services for disabled people could be provided by more than a dozen different organisations. These tended to be large, bureaucratic and remote, and consequently they found it difficult to respond to individual needs in a personalised way. Furthermore, there was considerable overlap as to the services provided, and demarcation lines were often blurred. As a consequence disabled people were passed from one department to another, or asked the same questions many times and this did little to enhance their quality of life.

Due to the complexities and overlapping services, it has often been suggested that 'co-ordination' is a major problem in providing services for disabled people. However, the real problem is not coordination, but as Wilding says (1982: 98), the consequences of services that had been built up around professional skills rather than client need.

> Services organised around professional skills are a tribute to the power of professionals in policy making. They also bear witness to a failure of professional responsibility. This is a failure to recognise that services organised around particular skills may be logical for professionals but may not meet the needs of clients and potential clients. *The real sufferers, for example, from the multiplicity of professionals actually or potentially involved in the care and rehabilitation of the physically handicapped are the handicapped.* (Emphasis added)

Finkelstein also agreed that the problem was not one of coordination, but one of the need for a change in the professional role – the professional must change from expert definer of need and/or gatekeeper of services and become a resource which a disabled person might use they choose:

> The endemic squabbles between rehabilitation workers about professional boundaries and the familiar farce of professional 'teamwork' can only be put to an end when all the workers and facilities in rehabilitation become resources in a process of self-controlled rehabilitation. (Finkelstein, 1981: 27)

Finkelstein (1999a; 1999b) called for an abandonment of professions allied to medicine in favour of professions allied to the community. These workers would replace existing services and service providers and be immersed within disability culture and politics, an essential ingredient in Finkelstein's view, if real change is to be achieved for and by disabled people. Thompson (2002: 717), in analysing the impact of the disabled people's movement, also calls for radical change:

> In some respects, this user participation movement has had the effect of challenging the complacency of a traditional model of professionalism based on the notion of 'we know best'. The notion of professionalism is an ambiguous one. It can refer to a commitment to high standards, to learning and development, to ethical practice and to accountability. In this regard, it is

compatible with emancipatory practice and the pursuit of social justice. However, it can also refer to elitism and relations of dominance and subordination, in which case it is far from compatible with social justice ... The challenge social work faces, therefore, is to develop forms of professionalism which are consistent with, and welcoming of, user participation and a commitment to equality and social justice – that is, professionalism based on partnership.

For social workers in local authority social services departments however, the problems are not only those of a service organised around narrow professional skills or even lack of coordination and teamwork, but also of working in departments where there is little or no recognition of the exercise of professional skills in working with disabled people. It could be argued that Seebohm (Department of Health and Social Security (1968) did not create generic departments, but specialist childcare ones, where the needs of children were met by trained professionals and other needs and obligations were met by unqualified staff, welfare assistants and the like, or passed on to occupational therapists employed by Social Services Departments. The Social Work Task Force and Reform Board have similarly made childcare their priority and adult social work services will presumably have to fit around them.

Despite this low priority, a disabled person can be confronted with many different professionals from health and social welfare agencies. A major problem for disabled people and their families therefore is not just a matter of which particular agency to approach, but also of which particular professional to contact. Furthermore, even when professionals are in contact, disabled people and their families are often unclear as to which department the professional represents and consequently what services may, or may not, be offered. To overcome this, the idea of a *named person* has variously been built into practice.

There are a number of problems related to this idea, particularly about whether the named person would in fact be the 'key worker' or simply someone given nominal responsibility, like the head of a special school. There is also the question about whether most professionals have sufficient knowledge and skills to act in this capacity. Both in terms of their strategic position and Finkelstein's principle of self-controlled rehabilitation, the disabled person is the most logical choice as both named person and key worker. The professional task, therefore, should not be to usurp the key worker position from the disabled person, but rather work with him or her to ensure that the required knowledge is acquired and thereby allay fears that a new profession of *named persons* could arise with its own career structure, salary increments and enhanced professional status.

There are a number of other problems to which the professional relationship can give rise. Some writers (McKnight, 1981; Davis, 2004) have suggested that the very relationship is itself disabling, and others (Fox, 1974; Robinson, 1978; Gibbs, 2004; Harris, 2004; Priestley, 2004) have pointed to the fact that very often professional definitions of need do not coincide with needs defined by disabled people themselves. Consequently, where professional and personal definitions of need conflict, the quality of life for disabled people is unlikely to be enhanced. Scott, who has written perceptively on the topic, stated that the professional:

> has been specially trained to give professional help to impaired people. He cannot use his expertise if those who are sent to him for assistance do not regard themselves as being impaired. Given this fact, it is not surprising that the doctrine has emerged among experts that truly effective rehabilitation and adjustment can occur only after the client has squarely faced and accepted the 'fact' that he is, indeed, 'impaired'. (Scott, 1970: 280)

It was not just in terms of acceptance of disability, but also in the assessment of needs and services that professionals sought to impose their definitions, though not always with total success. Thus, many disabled people have had their needs defined and purportedly met by professionalised welfare bureaucracies that very often do not provide the appropriate service in an acceptable fashion.

Hence there are organisational pressures, embedded in the structures of the welfare system, which have prevented social work practice from developing the radical approach that is necessary for working within a social model:

> The social model then, has had no real impact on professional practice, and social work has failed to meet disabled people's self-articulated needs. Twenty years ago [in the first edition of this book], I predicted that if social work was not prepared to change in terms of its practice towards disabled people it would eventually disappear altogether ... We can probably now announce the death of social work at least in relation to its involvement in the lives of disabled people. (Oliver, 2004: 25)

Seven years on from this prediction social work is surviving, but not flourishing, While that may seem to be an appropriate point at which to end, this death is a lingering one and for those individuals who are able to embrace the changes required, there are likely to be opportunities of working with disabled people within a citizenship approach, perhaps as professionals allied to communities. The final section of this chapter therefore considers the strategies that social workers may need to employ in order to practice with and alongside disabled people in their struggle to remove disabling barriers.

Some strategies for social work

While the traditional role of social workers with disabled people may be dying, there are aspects of professional social work that have the potential to be of use within a citizenship approach, but this is dependent upon the ideologies that inform practice. A profession built upon an expertise model such as medicine or law, which ignores the voices and experiences of those people they purport to serve, will do little to change the unequal and debilitating power relationships between the welfare state and disabled people. Neither will codes of ethics, based upon individualistic ideologies, help to achieve progress in the struggle against social barriers as they tend to value people despite, rather than because of, their difference. What is required is a form of professionalism that is capable of asserting itself in the face of oppressive social policies, but which does so with disabled people rather than for them. As noted in the last edition of this book a social work profession that might achieve this would need to add several features to its curriculum. As discussed throughout this book there has not been a great shift from individual interpretations of disability toward a focus on the cultural and societal barriers which disabled people with impairments face. The five points made in the last edition remain today, they do not make up an exhaustive list but still provide an important basis for a way forward, these follow.

First, disability equality training and disability studies would need to be integral to the education of social workers. Disability equality training is essential because of the depth to which negative assumptions about dependency and impairment are embedded in the culture of our society. Anti-disablist social work cannot be taught from textbooks alone as the hegemony of the individual model prevents even those who are aware of oppression from developing a full understanding of what is involved. This was seen in the debate concerning carers and the proposition that institutional care would provide a non-sexist solution to the problem of dependency (Finch, 1984). The construction of such an argument arises from an awareness and politicisation of the oppression of women, and while such theorising might be transferred to other issues such as racism or homophobia, the dominance of the individual model of disability prevents even the most politically aware people from transferring their understanding to the oppression of people with impairments. The struggle against disablism is not one of simply asserting equal rights, but of challenging basic concepts of normality. As Jenny Morris put it:

> I think that the challenge that it makes to the rest of society is absolutely fundamental. I just think it's extraordinary the changes that it's trying to bring about. The whole way that people think about themselves and about their impairment. These things are very, very significant and they are changing society very fundamentally. (Cited in Campbell and Oliver, 1996: 139)

In terms of the social work curriculum such an awareness raising exercise would not simply be aimed at the individual level of practitioners and students, but at the cultural assumptions that inform the design of the syllabus for degrees in social work. The focus on normality and deviancy through the inclusion of the study of human growth and development within this syllabus typifies the way in which, despite the exhortation of the social model within the context of anti-oppressive practice, social work education is still dominated by the theories based on the individual model of disability.

Although raising awareness is essential, it is insufficient to bring about an informed social work practice. What is also required is that social workers have a knowledge of the social model of disability that will inform their actions as practitioners and managers within a welfare system that itself has been seen to be oppressive. Social work practice will not progress unless it is modified to incorporate the social model of disability. This is not simply an academic debate for what we see is the individual model of disability causing service providers to ignore abuse of disabled children and adults. Second, it is insufficient to simply direct training at those who express an interest. The lesson is that disability equality training must include the majority of social workers and their managers, while recognising that the role of specialists is complex and must not be sacrificed. This can be achieved by the incorporation of disability studies as a central, even foundational aspect of the curriculum for social work education and continuing professional development. Disability studies should be on a par with childhood studies on all social work degrees.

In their inaugural conference in 2003, the Disability Studies Association stated that:

> Disability Studies is concerned with the inter-disciplinary development of an increasing body of knowledge and practice, which has arisen from the activities of the disabled people's movement, and which has come to be known as 'the social model of disability'. The social model of disability locates the changing character of disability, which is viewed as an important dimension of inequality, in the social and economic structure and culture of the society in which it is found, rather than in individual limitations.
>
> Disability Studies seeks to advance teaching, research and scholarship that is concerned with:
>
> - the analysis of disability and the exclusion of disabled people as a social consequence of impairment; and
> - the identification and development of strategies for fundamental social and political changes that are necessary for the creation of an inclusive society in which disabled people are full participants, and are guaranteed the same rights as non-disabled people.
>
> (Disability Studies Association, 2003)

Currently, only a few social work degrees in the United Kingdom teach disability studies and few social workers attend postgraduate courses on the subject. As a result, while many disability studies academics and researchers are developing the knowledge base and practice strategies that would be required to improve the lives of disabled people, they have too little impact on social work practice (Harris, 2003). As a consequence, social workers continue to make applications for their clients to enter residential and nursing homes, their managers continue to spend very large proportions of their budgets on such unwanted services, while local authorities continue to argue that they lack the funding for the services people actually want. If social workers and their managers are to act differently in their professional lives, they need to be educated differently.

Second, social workers and social service agencies need to give their full support to schemes designed to promote independent living, especially direct payments. There is evidence to suggest (Sapey and Pearson, 2002) that social workers regard people who opt for direct payments as opting out of the collective welfare system. Some social workers regard these people as no longer eligible for their support. There is also evidence to show that social workers actively discourage people from using direct payments as they see this as a loss of their budgets, and should they not be successful in this dissuasion, then they and their agencies will try to place restrictions of the use of the payments, indeed eligibility criteria itself might specifically be likely to increasingly become a barrier.

Social workers and their managers need to view direct payment schemes as an integral part of a collective approach to the provision of personal assistance. Implementing these schemes positively would provide social workers with the means of promoting independent living and helping disabled people to access mainstream economic and social life (Priestley, 1999).

Third, the most common area in which disputes will arise is that of assessment of need. While local authorities currently retain the right to determine the needs of individuals there will always be a level of conflict over the interpretation and assessment of need. This was discussed in detail in previous chapters and various strategies for practitioners to undertake assessments within a social model approach were proposed. At the core of this are the issues of empowerment and self-assessment. However, what may also be required is that social workers adopt a position of 'determined advocacy' in relation to supporting the rights of individual disabled people to participate and to define their own needs.

Determined advocacy implies not making judgements about whether the self-assessment of need is correct by some normative criteria, but to advocate for that assessment without reservation. This is not to relinquish any form of professional judgement or involvement with the individual concerned as the advice and experience of the social worker may be of immense value in helping disabled people develop strategies in their self-assessment. Rather it is to ensure that the social work role is not to act as yet another barrier to independent living – it is to enable rather than disable.

Fourth is the role of counselling in social work practice with disabled people. This is a matter that social workers often dispute as to whether it is part of their task, with some viewing it as the only therapeutic skill that they can genuinely possess while others consider it to be a specialist activity and not part of the administration of welfare. There are good arguments for both positions. Those who support the practice of counselling would suggest that social work is not simply a matter of administrating the delivery of material and personal services, but one of helping people who are failing to realise their potential within the social sphere of their lives to achieve their potential. As such counselling becomes a useful skill to either raise the consciousness of individuals or in a less radical manner, to help people understand the meanings of their own actions.

A counter to this argument is that because of the position that social workers occupy within the power structures of the welfare system, it would be wrong to employ skills that may blur the transparency with which their actions should be conducted, if they are to enable the full participation of their clients. This view may see counselling as a manipulative process or simply as a matter that should be kept quite separate from the provision of social services. To some extent both these arguments are conducted within an individual model of understanding of disability in which counselling is used to either help people come to terms with their impairment, or not, if it is seen as an inadequate response to the request for material help. From the perspective of the social model what is required is to evaluate the usefulness of counselling in the struggle to remove disabling barriers. One piece of research into what might constitute counselling in a social model of practice concluded that:

> The focus of counselling physically disabled people seems to be one of very consciously giving control back to the client or enabling the client to empower themselves through practical, emotional and social means. This is found to be necessary as many disabled people have had difficult and often painful experiences at the hands of the medical and allied professions or in their families or in interactions with the public at large. Due to their circumstances they have had to rely on others for their practical needs and sometimes the 'professionals' or family members have taken over the decision making for the disabled person. The result of feeling out of control, in a practical sense, has led to emotional difficulties for some disabled people. The

emotional cost for them of not feeling empowered is having low self-esteem, low self-confidence and a feeling of worthlessness. (Oliver, 1995: 275)

Thus, counselling can play a useful and necessary role in countering the impact of many of the disabling barriers that people with impairments face. While it would certainly be right for social workers to refuse to counsel people with the aim of getting them to accept the non-provision of material resources, it would be wrong to reject counselling per se.

Fifth, there is a need to rediscover the role of community social work within community care. The onset of care management has had the effect of neutralising social work as a radical activity. The development of procedures and regulations for the provision of services along with the limitation of the legitimate role of social work to this instrumental activity has curtailed many of the roles of social workers that were previously undisputed. Social work within local authorities tends to be viewed as a purely administrative process and one that might legitimately be undertaken by people with some other form of training. However, this would be to accept that the current organisation of disability services and of welfare in general is appropriate and that there is no need for it to be challenged from within the system.

Community social work has always meant working with and within communities to assist them to realise greater benefits from the welfare state and it is to these roles of advocacy and development that social work must return. The struggle against disability is a collective one as the solutions are social rather than individual. If social work is to be an effective ally in the struggle and to use its influence within the welfare state to alter and modify disability policies, it must do so from a position that is informed by its work with collective organisations of disabled people. It may, in Finkelstein's terms, need to become a profession allied to the community (Finkelstein 1999a; Finkelstein 1999b). Individual disabled people who are isolated from these developments may be in touch with social workers who can help by making them aware of the collective nature of their problems and by working with or supporting the development of a Centre for Independent Living. Social workers can also help organisations of disabled people to be heard in preference to the traditional organisations *for* the disabled that have established access to social service managements.

It is impossible and would be quite wrong to attempt to reproduce the instrumentalism of care management by giving a list of social work tasks that flow from an acceptance of the social model of disability. The issues that have been highlighted here are the most obvious and perhaps most urgent that need to be addressed by the social work establishment – its professional bodies, education providers and principal employers. It is only by examining and re-examining the implications of the social model analysis for the structures of social policy, the management of the welfare system and the actual practice of social work that social workers will be able to formulate a means of working that is meaningful and useful to disabled people as citizens, not clients.

CHAPTER OVERVIEW
- The first edition of this book was written in the hope that the social model of disability would provide a useful basis for constructing an effective social work practice with disabled people.
- Economic and political changes coupled with a less than inspired professional leadership of the social work profession has meant that many of earlier hopes have not materialised.
- The emergence of a strong and committed movement of disabled people based upon the social model of disability has meant that an enabling professional practice remains firmly on the agenda.
- The individual model of disability is so embedded in social work practice that in its current form this profession is unlikely to retain a role of working with disabled people as citizens.
- The citizenship approach to welfare seeks to fundamentally change the relationship that disabled people have with the welfare state and this also requires the administrators of welfare to fundamentally change.
- We hope that this book will be a vehicle for such a change and that those social workers who understand and appreciate the need for change will join in the struggle of the disabled people movement.

Point for reflection

Oliver (2004: 25) has argued that 'We can probably now announce the death of social work at least in relation to its involvement in the lives of disabled people.' Examine the curriculum of the social work course you undertook, or are undertaking, and decide how much is relevant, or not, to working with disabled people. What additional knowledge and skills do you think you would require that were/are not on this course? On completing this final exercise you should have the basis for identifying your own professional development needs.

Further resources

Oliver, M. and Barnes, C. (2012) *The New Politics of Disablement* (Basingstoke: Palgrave Macmillan).

Breakthrough UK is a disabled people's organisation which supports independent living particularly in relation to employment and conducts social model research and consultancy in all areas of independent living: www.breakthrough-uk.co.uk

Centre for Disability Research, Lancaster University has, since 2003, hosted the International Disability Studies conference and many of the papers presented are available on this site: www.lancs.ac.uk/cedr

Disability Studies Archive is an ever expanding collection of hundreds of papers which are not easily available elsewhere: www.leeds.ac.uk/disability-studies/archiveuk/index.html

References

ADASS (Association of Directors of Adult Social Services) (2009) *Social Work Task Force Call for Evidence: Response from the Association of Directors of Adult Social Services*. www.adass.org.uk/images/stories/ ADASS%20Sumbission%20to%20the%20Social%20Work%20Task force%201.6.09.pdf.

ADASS/Department of Health (2010) *The Future of Social Work in Adult Services*. www.dh.gov.uk/prod_consum_dh/groups/dh_digitalassets/ @dh/@en/@ps/documents/digitalasset/dh_114572.pdf.

Ahmad, W. (ed.) (2000) *Ethnicity, Disability and Chronic Illness*, Buckingham: Open University Press.

Albrecht, G. and Levy, J. (1981) 'Constructing Disabilities as Social problems', in G. Albrecht (ed.), *Cross National Rehabilitation Policies: A Sociological Perspective*, Beverly Hills: Sage.

Aldridge, J. and Becker, S. (1996) 'Disability Rights and the Denial of Young Carers: the Dangers of Zero-sum Arguments', *Critical Social Policy*, 16(3) pp. 55–76.

Allen, C., Milner, J. and Price, D. (2002) *Home is Where the Start Is*, Bristol: Policy Press.

Audit Commission (1986) *Making a Reality of Community Care*, London: HMSO.

Avante Consultancy (2006) *On Safe Ground – LGBT Disabled People and Community Groups*. www.leeds.ac.uk/disability-studies/archiveuk/ advante/On%20Safe%20Ground%20-%20lgbt%20disabled%20 people%20and%20community%20groups%85.pdf.

Avery, D. (1997) Message to disability research discussion group, RE: age onset of disability, 9th June: disability-research@mailbase.ac.uk.

Bailey, R. and Lee, P. (ed.) (1982) *Theory and Practice in Social Work*, Oxford: Blackwell.

Baistow, K. (1995) 'Liberation and Regulation? Some paradoxes of empowerment', *Critical Social Policy*, Issue 42, pp. 34–46.

Barnes, C. (1991) *Disabled People in Britain and Discrimination. A Case for Anti-Discrimination Legislation*, London: Hurst & Company.

Barnes, C., Jolly, D., Mercer, G., Pearson, C., Priestley, M. and Riddell, S. (2004) 'Developing Direct Payments: A Review of Policy Development in the UK', Paper at the Disability Studies: Putting Theory into Practice conference, Lancaster University, 26–28 July. http://www.lancs.

ac.uk/fass/events/disabilityconference_archive/2004/papers/jolly_pearson2004.pdf.

Barnes, C. and Mercer, G. (eds) (2004) *Implementing the Social Model of Disability: Theory and Research*, Leeds: The Disability Press.

Barnes, C., Mercer, G. and Morgan, H. (2001) *Creating Independent Futures: An Evaluation of Services Led by Disabled People Stage 3 Report*, Leeds: The Disability Press.

Barton, R. (1959) *Institutional Neurosis*, London: John Wright. http://contents.bjdd.net/oldPDFs/12_37to44.pdf.

BASW (British Association of Social Workers) (1982) *Guidelines for Social Work with the Disabled, Draft Paper*, London: BASW.

BASW (British Association of Social Workers) (1990) *Managing Care: The Social Work Task*, London: BASW.

BCODP (1987) Disabled People: Looking at Housing (Derbyshire: BCODP) www.leeds.ac.uk/disability-studies/archiveuk/BCODP/British%20Council%20of%20Organisations.pdf.

Beardshaw, V. (1993) ''Conductive Education: A Rejoinder', in J. Swain, V. Finkelstein, S. French and M. Oliver (eds) *Disabling Barriers – Enabling Environments*, London: Sage.

Begum, N., Hill, M. and Stevens, A. (eds) (1994) *Reflections: The Views of Black Disabled People on their Lives and on Community Care*, London: CCETSW.

Bell, L. and Klemz, A. (1981) *Physical Handicap*, Harlow: Longman.

Bennett, E. (2009) *What Makes my Family Stronger – A Report into What Makes Families with Disabled Children Stronger – Socially, Emotionally and Practically*, London: Contact a Family.

Beresford, P. (2004) 'Social Work and a Social Model of Madness and Distress: Developing a Viable Role for the Future', *Social Work & Social Sciences Review*, 12(2) pp. 59–73.

Blackburn, C. M., Spencer, N. J. and Read, J. M. (2010) 'Prevalence of Childhood Disability and the Characteristics and Circumstances of Disabled Children in the UK: Secondary Analysis of the Family Resources Survey', School of Health and Social Studies, University of Warwick. www.biomedcentral.com/content/pdf/1471-2431-10-21.pdf.

Blaxter, M. (1980) *The Meaning of Disability*, 2nd edn, London: Heinemann.

Blunden, R. and Ash, A. (2007) *No Place Like Home: Ordinary Residence, Discrimination and Disabled People*, London: VODG.

Booth, T. (1992) *Reasons for Admission to Part III Residential Homes*, London: National Council of Domiciliary Care Services.

Borsay, A. (2005) *Disability and Social Policy in Britain since 1750*, Basingstoke: Palgrave Macmillan.

Boswell, D. M. and Wingrove, J. M. (eds) (1974) *The Handicapped Person in the Community*, London: Tavistock.

Braye, S. and Preston-Shoot, M. (1997) *Practising Social Work Law,* 2nd edn, Basingstoke: Macmillan.

Brechin, A. and Liddiard, P. (1981) *Look at this Way: New Perspectives in Rehabilitation*, London: Hodder & Stoughton.

British Institute of Human Rights (2011) *Our Human Rights Stories*: 'Using The Human Rights Act to Challenge Adequate Community Care Services'. www.ourhumanrightsstories.org.uk/case-study/using-human-rights-act-challenge-failure-provide-adequate-community-care-services.

British Medical Association (2010) 'Responding to Patient Requests Relating to Assisted Suicide: Guidance for Doctors in England, Wales and Northern Ireland', www.bma.org.uk/images/assistedsuicide guidancejuly2010_tcm41-198675.pdf.

Brown, H. and Craft, A. (eds) (1989) *Thinking the Unthinkable: Papers on Sexual Abuse and People with Learning Difficulties*, London: Family Planning Association.

Brown, H. (2003) Safeguarding adults and children with disabilities against abuse, Strasbourg: Council of Europe.

Buckle, J. (1971) *Work and Housing of Impaired People in Great Britain*, London: HMSO.

Buckner, L. and Yeandle, S. (2007) *Valuing Carers – Calculating the Value of Unpaid Care*, London: Carers UK.

Burleigh, M. (1996) 'Spending Lives: Psychiatry, Society and the 'Euthanasia' Programme', in M. Burleigh (ed.) *Confronting the Nazi Past*, London: Collins & Brown.

Burleigh, M. (2000) *The Third Reich: A New History*, Basingstoke: Macmillan.

Bury, M. (1996) 'Defining and Researching Disability: Challenges and Responses', in C. Barnes and G. Mercer (eds) *Exploring the Divide: Illness and Disability*, Leeds: The Disability Press.

Campbell, J. (2003) *Assisted Dying and Human Value*, Select Committee on the Assisted Dying for the Terminally Ill Bill [HL], www.leeds.ac.uk/disability-studies/archiveuk/Campbell/assisted dying.pdf.

Campbell, J. and Oliver, M. (eds) (1996) *Disability Politics*, London: Routledge.

Care Quality Commission (2010) www.cqc.org.uk/newsandevents/news stories.cfm?widCall1=customWidgets.content_view_1&cit_id=35862.

Cavet, J. (1999) *People Don't Understand: Children, Young People and their Families Living with a Hidden Disability*, London: National Children's Bureau.

CCETSW (Central Council for Education and Training in Social Work) (1974) *Social Work: People with Handicaps Need Better Trained Workers*, London: CCETSW.

CCETSW (Central Council for Education and Training in Social Work) (1989) *Requirements and Regulations for the Diploma in Social Work*, London: CCETSW.

Chief Inspectors (2005) *Safeguarding Children: The Second Joint Chief Inspectors' Report on Arrangements to Safeguard Children*, London: Commission for Social Care Inspection.

Chief Inspectors (2008) *Safeguarding Children, The THIRD joint Chief Inspectors' Report on Arrangements to Safeguard Children*, London: Commission for Social Care Inspection.

Children's Act (1989) www.legislation.gov.uk/ukpga/1989/41/contents.

Clark, F. le Gros (1969) *Blinded in War: A Model for the Welfare of all Handicapped People*, London: Wayland.

Clarke, H. and McKay, S. (2008) 'Exploring Disability, Family Formation and Break-up: Reviewing the Evidence', Research Report No 514, London: DWP) http://research.dwp.gov.uk/asd/asd5/rports2007-2008/rrep514.pdf.

Clark, L. (2006) 'A Comparative Study on the Effects of Community Care – Charging Policies for Personal Assistance Users', unpublished MA dissertation.

Clements, L. and Read, J. (2003) *Disabled People and European Human Rights*, Bristol: Policy Press.

Crawford, K. and Walker, J. (2008) *Social Work with Older People*, Exeter: Learning Matters Ltd.

Croft, S. (1986) 'Women, Caring and the Recasting Of need – A Feminist Reappraisal', *Critical Social Policy*, 16, pp. 23–39.

Crow, L. (1996) 'Including All of Our Lives: Renewing the Social Model of Disability', in C. Barnes and G. Mercer (eds) *Exploring the Divide*, Leeds: The Disability Press.

Crow, L. (2010) 'Resistance – which way the future?', *Coalition*, January, Manchester: Manchester Coalition of Disabled People.

Crown Prosecution Service (2006) *Guidance on Prosecuting Cases of Disability Hate Crime*, London: CPS. www.cps.gov.uk/publications/docs/disability_hate_crime_guidance.pdf.

Crown Prosecution Service (2010) Policy for Prosecutors in Respect of Cases of Encouraging or Assisting Suicide. www.cps.gov.uk/publications/prosecution/assisted_suicide_policy.html.

CSCI (Commission for Social Care Inspection) (2009) *The State of Social Care in England 2007–08*. http://webarchive.nationalarchives.gov.uk/20100611090857/www.cqc.org.uk/_db/_documents/SOSC08%20Report%2008_Web.pdf.

Dalley, G. (1996) *Ideologies of Caring*, London: Macmillan.

Davey, V. *et al.* (2007) *Direct Payments: A National Survey of Direct Payments Policy and Practice*, London: Personal Social Services Research Unit, London School of Economics and Political Science.

Davis, K. (1981) '28–38 Grove Road: Accommodation and Care in a Community Setting', in A. Brechin, P. Liddiard and J. Swain (eds) *Handicap in a Social World*, London: Hodder & Stoughton.

Davis, K. (1984) *Notes on the development of the Derbyshire Centre for Integrated Living.* www.leeds.ac.uk/disability-studies/archiveuk/DavisK/earlydcil.pdf.

Davis, K. (1990) 'A Social Barriers Model of Disability: Theory into Practice: The Emergence of the "Seven Needs"', Paper prepared for the Derbyshire Coalition of Disabled People: February, 1990. www.leeds.ac.uk/disability-studies/archiveuk/DavisK/davis-social%20barriers.pdf.

Davis, K. (2004) 'The Crafting of Good Clients' in J. Swain, S. French, C. Barnes and C. Thomas (eds) *Disabling Barriers – Enabling Environments,* 2nd edition, London: Sage.

Dawson, C. (2000) *Independent Success: Implementing Direct Payments,* York: Joseph Rowntree Foundation.

Department for Education and Skills (2001) Special Educational Needs Code of Practice http://media.education.gov.uk/assets/files/pdf/s/sen%20code%20of%20practice.pdf.

Department for Education (2007) *Aiming High for Disabled Children: Better Support for Families.* www.education.gov.uk/childrenandyoungpeople/sen/ahdc/b0070490/aiming-high-for-disabled-children-ahdc.

Department for Education (2010a) *Children with Special Educational Needs 2010: An Analysis 19 October 2010.* www.education.gov.uk/rsgateway/DB/STA/t000965/osr25-2010.pdf.

Department for Education (2010b) *Building a Safe and Confident Future: One Year On – Detailed Proposals from the Social Work Reform Board.* www.education.gov.uk/publications/standard/publicationDetail/Page1/DFE-00602-2010.

Department for Education (2011a) *Support and Aspiration: A New Approach to Special Educational Needs and Disability.* www.education.gov.uk/publications/eOrderingDownload/Green-Paper-SEN.pdf.

Department for Education (2011b) *Short Breaks for carers of Disabled Children Advice for Local Authorities.* http://media.education.gov.uk/assets/files/pdf/s/short%20breaks%20-%20advice%20for%20local%20authorities.pdf.

Department of Health and Social Security (1968) *Report of the Committee on Local Authority and Allied Social Services,* Seebohm Report, London: HMSO.

Department of Health (1998) *Modernising Social Services: Promoting Independence, Improving Protection, Raising Standards,* London: Department of Health.

Department of Health (1989) *Caring for People – Community Care in the Next Decade and Beyond,* London: HMSO.

Department of Health (2000) *A Quality Strategy for Social Care,* London: Department of Health.

Department of Health (2002) *Requirements for Social Work Training,* London: Department of Health.

Department of Health (2003) *Fair Access to Care Services*, London: Department of Health) www.dh.gov.uk/prod_consum_dh/groups/dh_digitalassets/@dh/@en/documents/digitalasset/dh_4019641.pdf.

Department of Health (2006) *White Paper, Our Health Our Care Our Say.* http://webarchive.nationalarchives.gov.uk/+/www.dh.gov.uk/en/Publicationsandstatistics/Publications/PublicationsPolicyAndGuidance/DH_4127453.

Department of Health (2007) *Putting People First.* www.dh.gov.uk/en/Publicationsandstatistics/Publications/PublicationsPolicyAndGuidance/DH_081118.

Department of Health (2008) *Putting People First – Transforming Adult Social Care.* www.dh.gov.uk/en/Publicationsandstatistics/Lettersand circulars/LocalAuthorityCirculars/DH_081934.

Department of Health (2010a) Prioritising need in the context of *Putting People First*: A whole system approach to eligibility for social care *Guidance on Eligibility Criteria for Adult Social Care, England 2010* Ch. 3 p. 11 www.dh.gov.uk/prod_consum_dh/groups/dh_digitalassets/@dh/@en/@ps/documents/digitalasset/dh_113155.pdf.

Department of Health (2010b) *Practical Approaches to Co-production.* www.dh.gov.uk/prod_consum_dh/groups/dh_digitalassets/@dh/@en/@ps/documents/digitalasset/dh_121669.pdf.

Department of Health (2010c) 'Equity and Excellence: Liberating the NHS' http://www.dh.gov.uk/prod_consum_dh/groups/dh_digitalassets/@dh/@en/@ps/documents/digitalasset/dh_117794.pdf.

Department for Work and Pensions (2010) 'About the ILF'. www.dwp.gov.uk/ilf/about-ilf/.

Department for Work and Pensions (2011) Welfare Reform Bill. www.dwp.gov.uk/policy/welfare-reform/legislation-and-key-documents/welfare-reform-bill-2011/index.shtml#main.

Despouy, L. (1993) *Human Rights and Disability*, New York: United Nations Economic and Social Council.

Direct Gov (2010) 'Support for Disabled Parents'. www.direct.gov.uk/en/DisabledPeople/Disabledparents/DG_10037844.

Disability Now, (2010) The Hate Crime Dossier webpage. http://www.disabilitynow.org.uk/the-hate-crime-dossier?searchterm=hate+crime.

Disability Discrimination (undated) www.disability.discrimination.com/pages/home/disability-discrimination-law/the-meaning-of-disability.php.

Disability Rights Commission (2006) *Whose Risk is it Anyway?* http://www.leeds.ac.uk/disability-studies/archiveuk/DRC/DD_Risk_Paper.pdf.

Disability Studies Association (2003) *2003 Conference Archive Home* www.lancs.ac.uk/fass/events/disabilityconference_archive/2003/.

Doyal, L. (1980) *The Political Economy of Health*, London: Pluto Press.

Dunning, J. (2011) 'Bureaucracy is Damaging Personalisation, Social Workers Say'. Community Care (online), 25 May. www.community care.co.uk/Articles/2011/05/25/116867/bureaucracy-is-damaging-personalisation-social-workers-say.htm.

Ellis, K. (1993) *Squaring the Circle: user and carer participation in needs assessment*, York: Joseph Rowntree Foundation.

Ermish, J. and Murphy, M. (2006) *Changing Household and Family Structures and Complex Living Arrangements*, Swindon: ESRC.

Equality and Human Rights Commission (EHRC) (2010) *The Essential Guide to the Public Sector Equality Duty*. www.equalityhumanrights.com/uploaded_files/EqualityAct/PSED/essential_guide_guidance.pdf.

Equality and Human Rights Commission (EHRC) (2011) *Respect for Your Family and Private Life*. www.equalityhumanrights.com/human-rights/what-are-human-rights/the-human-rights-act/respect-for-your-private-and-family-life/.

Equal Opportunities Commission (1982) *Caring for the Elderly and Handicapped*, London: Equal Opportunities Commission.

Evans, A. MP (1947) 'National Assistance Act debate', Hansard, 24 November 1947. http://hansard.millbanksystems.com/commons/1947/nov/24/national-assistance-bill.

Evans, A. MP quoted in Silburn, R. (1983) 'Social Assistance and Social Welfare: the Legacy of the Poor Law', in P. Bean and S. MacPherson (eds), *Approaches to Welfare*, London: Routledge & Kegan Paul.

Evans, J. (2002) *Independent Living Movement in the UK*. www.leeds.ac.uk/disability-studies/archiveuk/evans/Version%202%20Independent%20Living%20Movement%20in%20the%20UK.pdf.

Evans, J. (2006) 'The Importance of CILs In Our Movement', presentation at the Puerta Valencia Hotel, 2 November 2006, http://www.leeds.ac.uk/disability-studies/archiveuk/evans/Valencia%20CIL%20Presentation%20john.pdf.

Felce, D. and Perry, J. (1997) 'Quality of Life: The Scope of the Term and its Breadth of Measurement', in R. Brown, R. (ed.) *Quality of Life for People with Disabilities*, 2nd edn, Cheltenham: Stanley Thornes Publishers Ltd.

Fiedler, B. (1988) *Living Options Lottery*, London: King's Fund Centre.

Fiedler, B. (1991) *Tracking Success: Testing Services for People with Severe Physical and Sensory Disabilities*, London: King's Fund Centre.

Finch, J. (1984) 'Community Care: developing non-sexist alternatives', in *Critical Social Policy*, 9, pp. 6–18.

Fine, A. and Ache, M. (eds) (1988) *Women with Disabilities*, Philadelphia: Temple University Press.

Finkelstein, V. (1972) *The Psychology of Disability* (print version from original audio tape transcript of talk). www.leeds.ac.uk/disability-studies/archiveuk/finkelstein/01%20-%20Talk%20to%20GPs.pdf.

Finkelstein, V. (1980) *Attitudes and Disabled People: Issues for Discussion*, New York: World Rehabilitation Fund.

Finkelstein, V. (1981) *Disability and professional attitudes*. RADAR (1981) Conference Proceedings. NAIDEX '81 21–24 October 1981. http://www.leeds.ac.uk/disability-studies/archiveuk/finkelstein/Professional%20Attitudes.pdf.

Finkelstein, V. (1991) 'Disability: An Administrative Challenge? (The Health and Welfare Heritage)', in M. Oliver (ed.) *Social Work Disabled People and Disabling Environments*, London: Jessica Kingsley.

Finkelstein, V. (1999a) *Professions Allied to the Community (PACs)*, [http://www.leeds.ac.uk/disability-studies/archiveuk/index.html].

Finkelstein, V. (1999b) *Professions Allied to the Community: The Disabled People's Trade Union*, http://www.leeds.ac.uk/disability-studies/archiveuk/index.html.

Finkelstein, V. and Stuart, O. (1996) 'Developing new services', in G. Hales (ed.), *Beyond Disability*, London: Sage.

Fox, A. M. (1974) *They get this training but they don't really know how you feel*, London: RADAR.

Friedlander, H. (1995) The Origins of Nazi Genocide from Euthanasia to the Final Solution, Chapel Hill: University of North Carolina Press.

Freire, P. (1972) *Pedagogy of the Oppressed*, Harmondsworth: Penguin.

Froggett, L. and Sapey, B. (1997) 'Communication, Culture and Competence in Social Work Education', *Social Work Education*, 16(1) pp. 41–53.

Gallagher, H. (1990) *By Trust Betrayed, Patients Physicians and the Licence to Kill in the Third Reich*, New York: Henry Holt.

General Social Care Council (GSCC) (2005) *Specialist Standards and Requirements (Adult Services)*, London: GSCC.

General Social Care Council (GSCC) (2008) *Social Work at Its Best – A Statement of Social Work Roles and Tasks for the 21st Century*. http://www.gscc.org.uk/cmsFiles/Policy/Roles%20and%20Tasks.PDF.

Gibbs, D. (2004) 'Social Model Services: an oxymoron?' in, C. Barnes and G. Mercer (eds) *Disability Policy and Practice: Applying the Social Model*, Leeds: The Disability Press.

Gibson, S. (2006) 'Beyond a "culture of silence": inclusive education and the liberation of "voice". *Disability and Society* 21(4) pp. 315–29.

Glasby, J. and Littlechild, R. (2009) *Direct Payments and Personal Budgets: Putting Personalisation into Practice*, Bristol: Policy Press.

Gleeson, B. (1999) *Geographies of Disability*, London: Routledge.

Goffman, E. (1961) *Asylums*, New York: Doubleday.

Gooding, C. (1996) *Blackstone's Guide to the Disability Discrimination Act 1995*, London: Blackstone Press.

Gooding, C. (2003) 'The Disability Discrimination Act: Winners and Losers', paper presented at *Working Futures* seminar, University of Sunderland, 3–5 December.

Goodinge, S. (2000) *A Jigsaw of Services: Inspection of services to support disabled parents in their parenting role*, London: Department of Health.

Griffiths, M. (2006) 'Sex: Should We All Be At It?' Sociology Dissertation University of Leeds, www.leeds.ac.uk/disability-studies/archiveuk/griffiths/dissertation.pdf.

Griffiths, R. (1988) *Community Care: Agenda for Action*, London: HMSO.

Guelke, J. (2003) 'Road-kill on the Information Highway: Repetitive Strain Injury in the Academy', *The Canadian Geographer*, 47(4) pp. 386–99.

Hanks, J. and Hanks, L. (1980) 'The Physically Handicapped in Certain Non-occidental Societies', in W. Phillips and J. Rosenberg (eds) *Social Scientists and the Physically Handicapped*, London: Arno Press.

Hanvey, C. (1981) *Social Work with Mentally Handicapped People*, London: Heinemann.

Harris, A. (1971) *Handicapped and Impaired in Great Britain*, London: HMSO.

Harris, J. (1995) *The Cultural Meaning of Deafness*, Aldershot: Averbury.

Harris, J. (1997) *Deafness and The Hearing*, Birmingham: Venture Press.

Harris, J. (2003) 'Ostrich Politics: Exploring the Place of Social Care in Disability Studies', paper presented at the Disability Studies: Theory, Policy and Practice conference, Lancaster University, September 4–6. http://www.lancs.ac.uk/fass/events/disabilityconference_archive/2003/papers/harris2003.pdf.

Harris, J. (2004) 'Incorporating the Social Model into Outcome-Focused Social Care Practice with Disabled People', in C. Barnes and G. Mercer (eds) *Disability Policy and Practice: Applying the Social Model*, Leeds: The Disability Press.

Hemingway, L. (2011) *Disabled People and Housing: Choices, Opportunities and Barriers*, Bristol: Policy Press.

Holdsworth, L. (1991) *Empowerment Social Work with Physically Disabled People*, Norwich: Social Work Monographs.

Holman, B. (1993) *A New Deal for Social Welfare*, Oxford: Lion.

Howe, D. (1987) *An Introduction to Social Work Theory*, Aldershot: Wildwood House.

Hunter S. and Ritchie P. (eds) (2007) *Co-production and Personalization in Social Care*, London: Jessica Kingsley.

iese (2011) Care Funding Calculator. www.southeastiep.gov.uk.

Illich, I. (1975) *Medical Nemesis: The Expropriation of Health*, London: Marion Boyars.

Imrie, R. (2003) *The Impact of Part M on the Design of New Housing*, Egham: Royal Holloway University of London.

Integration alliance (1992) *The Inclusive Education System: A National Policy for Fully Integrated Education.* www.leeds.ac.uk/disability-studies/archiveuk/integration%20alliance/inclusive%20ed%20system.pdf.

IPPR (2007) *DISABILITY 2020: Opportunities for the full and equal citizenship of disabled people in Britain in 2020*, London: IPPR.

Jacques, M. (1997) 'Les enfants de Marx et de Coca-Cola', *New Statesman*, 28 November, pp. 34–6.

Kanter, A. (2007) 'The Promise and Challenge of the United Nations Convention on the rights of Persons with Disabilities', *Syracuse Journal of International Law and Commerce*, 34(2), pp. 287–322.

Katbamna, S., Bhakta, P. and Parker, G. (2000) 'Perceptions of disability and care-giving relationships in South Asian communities', in W. Ahmad (ed.) *Ethnicity, Disability and Chronic Illness*, Buckingham: Open University Press.

Keith, L. and Morris, J. (1995) 'Easy Targets: A Disability Rights Perspective on the "Children as Carers" Debate', *Critical Social Policy*, 15(2/3) pp. 36–57.

Kelly, L. (1992) 'The Connections between Disability and Child Abuse: A Review of the Research Evidence', *Child Abuse Review*, 1(3) pp. 157–67.

Kennedy, M. (1989) 'The Abuse of Deaf Children', *Child Abuse Review*, 3(1), pp. 3–7.

Kitson, D. and Clawson, R. (2007) 'Safeguarding Children with Disabilities', in K. Wilson and A. James (eds) *The Child Protection Handbook*, 3rd edn, London: Elsevier.

Kuhn, T. (1962) *The Structure of Scientific Revolutions*, Chicago: University of Chicago Press.

Langan, M. (1990) 'Community Care in the 1990s: the Community Care White Paper: "Caring for People"', *Critical Social Policy*, Issue 29, pp. 58–70.

Lago, C. and Smith, B. (eds) (2003) *Anti-discriminatory Counselling Practice*, London: Sage.

Law Commission (2011) *Adult Social Care: Presented to Parliament pursuant to section 3(2) of the Law Commissions Act 1965*. Law Com No 326. www.justice.gov.uk/lawcommission/docs/lc326_adult_social_care.pdf.

Le Grand, J. and Bartlett, W. (eds.) (1993) *Quasi-Markets and Social Policy*, Basingstoke: Macmillan.

Lenney, M. and Sercombe, H. (2002) ' "Did You See That Guy in the Wheelchair Down the Pub?" Interactions across Difference in a Public Place', *Disability & Society*, 17(1) pp. 5–18.

Lenny, J. (1993) 'Do Disabled People Need Counselling?' in J. Swain, V. Finkelstein, S. French and M. Oliver (eds) *Disabling Barriers – Enabling Environments*, London: Sage.

Leonard, P. (1966) 'The Challenge of Primary Prevention', *Social Work Today*, 6 October.

Lifton, R. J. (2000) *The Nazi Doctors – Medical Killing and the Psychology of Genocide*, New York: Basic Books.

MacFarlane, A. (1994) 'On Becoming an Older Disabled Woman', *Disability and Society*, 9(2) pp. 255–6.

MacFarlane, A. and Laurie, L. (1996) *Demolishing Special Needs* (Derbyshire: BCODP.

Marchant, R. and Page, M. (1992) *Bridging the Gap*, London: NSPCC.

Martin, J., Meltzer, H. and Elliot, D. (1988) *The Prevalence of Disability among Adults*, London: HMSO.

McConnell, H. and Wilson, B. (2007) *Focus on the Family*, London: Office for National Statistics.

McDonald, E. v Royal Borough of Kensington & Chelsea. Neutral Citation Number [2010] EWCA Civ 1109. www.bailii.org/ew/cases/EWCA/Civ/2010/1109.html.

McKnight, J. (1981) 'Professionalised Service and Disabled Help', in A. Brechin, P. Liddiard and J. Swain (eds) *Handicap in a Social World*, London: Hodder & Stoughton.

Merton, R. (1957) *Social Theory and Social Structure*, New York: Free Press.

Middleton, L. (1992) *Children First: Working with Children and Disability*, Birmingham: Venture Press.

Middleton, L. (1995) *Making a Difference: Social Work with Disabled Children*, Birmingham: Venture Press.

Middleton, L. (1997) *The Art of Assessment: Practitioners Guide*, Birmingham: Venture Press.

Middleton, L. (1999) *Disabled Children: Challenging Social Exclusion*, London: Blackwell Science.

Miller, E. and Gwynne, G. (1972) *A Life Apart*, London: Tavistock.

Moore, M., Skelton, J. and Patient, M. (2000) *Enabling Future Care*, Birmingham: Venture Press.

Morris, J. (1989) *Able Lives: Women's Experience of Paralysis*, London: The Women's Press.

Morris, J. (1991) *Pride against Prejudice*, London: Women's Press.

Morris, J. (1993a) *Independent Lives: Community Care and Disabled People*, Basingstoke: Macmillan.

Morris, J. (1993b) *Community Care or Independent Living*, York: Joseph Rowntree Foundation.

Morris, J. (1997a) *Community Care: Working in Partnership with Service Users*, Birmingham: Venture Press.

Morris, J. (1997b) 'Gone Missing? Disabled Children Living Away from their Families', *Disability & Society*, 12(2) pp. 241–58.

Morris, J. (1998) *Still Missing?*, London: Who Cares? Trust.

Morris, J. (2002) *A Lot To Say*, London: Scope.

Morris, J. and Wates, M. (2006) *Supporting Disabled Parents and Parents with Additional Support Needs*, Bristol: Policy Press/SCIE.

Mortier, K., Desimpel, L., De Schauwer, E. and Van Hove, G. (2011) 'I Want Support Not Comments: Children's Perspective on Supports in their Life', *Disability and Society* 26(2) pp. 207–22.

Mostert, M.P. (2002) 'Useless Eaters: Disability as Genocidal Marker in Nazi Germany', *Journal of Special Education*, 36, 155–68.

Neimeyer, R. A. and Anderson, A. (2002) 'Meaning Reconstruction Theory', in N. Thompson (ed.) *Loss and Grief*, Basingstoke: Palgrave Macmillan.

NHS Information Centre (2010) *Survey of Carers in Households 2009/10*. www.ic.nhs.uk/webfiles/publications/009_Social_Care/carer survey0910/Survey_of_Carers_in_Households_2009_10_England.pdf.

NHS Information Centre (2011a) Community Care Statistics 2009–10: Social Services Activity, England. www.ic.nhs.uk/webfiles/publications/009_Social_Care/carestats0910asrfinal/Community_Care_Statistics_200910_Social_Services_Activity_Report_England.pdf.

NHS Information Centre (2011b) Personal Social Services expenditure and unit costs: England – 2009–10 – Final Council Data http://www.ic.nhs.uk/webfiles/publications/009_Social_Care/pss0910 expfinal/pss0910expfinal_update_070311/Personal_Social_Services_Expenditure_Report%202009_10.pdf.

NHS Information Centre (2011c) Abuse of Vulnerable Adults in England October 2009 – March 2010. Experimental Statistics. www.ic.nhs.uk/webfiles/publications/009_Social_Care/ava0910/Abuse_of_Vulnerable_Adults_report_2009-10.pdf.

Nissel, M. and Bonnerjea, L. (1982) *Family Care of the Handicapped Elderly: Who Pays?*, London: Policy Studies Institute.

Not Dead Yet UK (2011) www.notdeadyetuk.org/page12.html.

Nowak, M. (2008) *Interim Report of the Special Rapporteur on Torture and Other Cruel, Inhuman or Degrading Treatment or Punishment*, New York: United Nations.

NSPCC (2003) *'It doesn't happen to disabled children': child protection and disabled children*. Report of the National Working Group on Child Protection and Disability, London: NSPCC.

O'Connell, P. (2005) ' "A Better Future?" Young adults with complex physical and communication needs in mainstream education.' Presented by Dawn Seals, BERA, at the University of Glamorgan, 17 September. www.leeds.ac.uk/disability-studies/archiveuk/o%27connell/oconnellp%20a%20better%20future%20bera%202005.pdf.

Office for Disability Issues (2010) *Disability Facts and Figures*. www.odi.gov.uk/disability-statistics-and-research/disability-facts-and-figures.php.

Office for National Statistics (ONS) (2001) www.statistics.gov.uk/cci/nugget.asp?id=458.

Office for National Statistics (ONS) (2004) *Social Trends No 34*, London.

Office for National Statistics (ONS) (2009) www.statistics.gov.uk/cci/nugget.asp?id=1264.

Office for National Statistics (ONS) (2010) Social Trends 40 No. 40 – 2010 edition Chapter 2 Households and families www.statistics.gov.uk/downloads/theme_social/Social-Trends40/ST40_Ch02.pdf.

Oliver, J. (1982) 'Community Care: Who Pays?' *New Society*, 24 March.

Oliver, J. (1995) 'Counselling Disabled People: A Counsellor's Perspective', *Disability & Society*, 10(3) pp. 261–79.

Oliver, M. (1982) *Disablement in Society*, Milton Keynes: Open University Press.

Oliver, M. (1983) *Social Work with Disabled People*, Basingstoke: Macmillan.

Oliver, M. (1990) *The Politics of Disablement*, Basingstoke: Macmillan.

Oliver, M. (ed.) (1991) *Social Work, Disabled People and Disabling Environments*, London: Jessica Kingsley.

Oliver, M. (1996) *Understanding Disability, From Theory to Practice*, Basingstoke: Macmillan.

Oliver, M. (2004) 'The Social Model in Action: If I Had a Hammer', in C. Barnes and G. Mercer (eds) *Implementing the Social Model of Disability: Theory and Research*, Leeds: The Disability Press.

Oliver, M. and Bailey, P. (2002) 'Report on the Application of the Social Model of Disability to the Services provided by Birmingham City Council', unpublished.

Oliver, M. and Barnes, C. (2012) *The New Politics of Disablement*, Basingstoke: Palgrave Macmillan.

Oliver. M, and Sapey, B. (1999) *Social Work with Disabled People*, 2nd edn, Basingstoke: Macmillan.

Oliver, M. and Sapey, B. (2006) *Social Work with Disabled People*, 3rd edn, Basingstoke: Palgrave Macmillan.

Oliver, M. and Zarb, G. (1992) *Greenwich Personal Assistance Schemes: An Evaluation*, London: Greenwich Association of Disabled People.

Philips, J., Ray, M. and Marshall, M. (2006) *Social Work With Older People* (British Association of Social Workers (BASW) Practical Social Work) (Practical Social Work).

Philips, T. (2007) *Fairness and Freedom: The Final Report of the Equalities Review*, London: Equalities Review.

Piggot, L. (2011) 'Prosecuting Disability Hate Crime: A Disabling Solution?', *People, Place & Policy Online*, pp. 5/1, pp. 25–34. http://extra.shu.ac.uk/ppp-online/issue_1_130411/issue_downloads/disability_hate_crime_solution.pdf.

Powles, J. (1973) 'On the Limitations of Modern Medicine', *Science, Medicine and Man*, 1.

Priestley, M. (1999) *Disability Politics and Community Care*, London: Jessica Kingsley.

Priestley, M. (2003) *Disability: A Life Course Approach*, Cambridge: Polity Press.

Priestley, M. (2004) 'Tragedy Strikes Again! Why Community Care Still Poses a Problem for Integrated Living' in J. Swain, S. French, C. Barnes and C. Thomas (eds) *Disabling Barriers – Enabling Environments*, 2nd edn, London: Sage.

Prime Minister's Strategy Unit (2005) *Improving the Life Chances of Disabled People*. www.cabinetoffice.gov.uk/strategy/work_areas/disability.aspx.

Read, J. (2000) *Disability, the Family and Society: Listening to Mothers*, Buckingham: Open University Press.

Read, J. and Clements, L. (2001) *Disabled Children and the Law: research and good practice*, London: Jessica Kingsley.

Reeve, D. (2000) 'Oppression within the counselling room', *Disability & Society* 15(4) pp. 669–82.

Reeve, D. (2002) 'Negotiating Psycho-emotional Dimensions of Disability and their Influence on Identity Constructions', *Disability & Society*, 17(5) pp. 493–508.

Reeve, D. (2004) 'Counselling and disabled people: help or hindrance?' in J. Swain, S. French, C. Barnes and C. Thomas (eds) *Disabling Barriers – Enabling Environments*, 2nd edn, London: Sage.

Residential Forum (2010) *Vision Statement*. www.residentialforum.com/residential_forum_vision_statement.html.

Roberts, P. (1994) 'Theoretical Models of Physiotherapy', *Physiotherapy*, 80(6): 361–6.

Robinson, T. (1978) *In Worlds Apart: Professionals and their Clients in the Welfare State*, London: Bedford Square Press.

Roith, A. (1974) 'The Myth of Parental Attitudes', in D. M. Boswell and J. M. Wingrove (eds) *The Handicapped Person in the Community*, London: Tavistock.

Roulstone, A. and Mason-Bish, H. (2012) *Disablist Hate Crime and Violence*, London: Routledge.

Roulstone, A. and Thomas, P. (2009) *Hate Crime and Disabled People*, Manchester: Equality and Human Rights Commission and Breakthrough UK.

Roulstone, A., Thomas, P. and Balderston, S. (2011) 'Between Hate and Vulnerability: Unpacking the British Criminal Justice System's construction of Disablist Hate Crime', *Disability and Society* 26(3) pp. 351–64.

Roulstone, A. and Warren, J. (2006) 'Applying a Barriers Approach to Monitoring Disabled People's Employment: Implications for the Disability Discrimination Act 2005', *Disability and Society* 21(2) pp. 115–31.

Runswick-Cole, K. (2008) 'Between a Rock and a Hard Place: Parents' Attitudes to the Inclusion of Children with Special Educational Needs in Mainstream and Special Schools', *British Journal of Special Education*, 35(3) pp. 73–180.

Ryan, J. and Thomas, F. (1980) *The Politics of Mental Handicap*, Harmondsworth, Penguin.

Salman, S. (2010) 'Caught in a Trap: Disabled People Can't Move Out of Care', *Guardian*, 13 October.

Salzberger-Wittenberg, I. (1970) *Psycho-Analytic Insights and Relationships: A Kleinian Approach*, London: Routledge & Kegan Paul.

Sapey, B. (1993) 'Community Care: Reinforcing the Dependency of Disabled People', *Applied Community Studies*, 1(3), pp. 21–29.

Sapey, B. (1995) 'Disabling Homes: A Study of the Housing Needs of Disabled People in Cornwall', *Disability and Society*, 10(1), pp. 71–85.

Sapey, B. (2004) 'Practice for What? The Use of Evidence in Social Work with Disabled People', in D. Smith (ed.) *Evidence-based Practice and Social Work*, London: Jessica Kingsley.

Sapey, B. and Hewitt, N. (1991) 'The Changing Context of Social Work Practice', in M. Oliver (ed.) *Social Work, Disabled People and Disabling Barriers*, London: Jessica Kingsley.

Sapey, B. and Pearson, J. (2002) *Direct Payments in Cumbria: An Evaluation of their Implementation*. www.lancs.ac.uk/cedr/activities/268/.

Sapey, B., Turner, R. and Orton, S. (2004) *Access to Practice: Overcoming the Barriers to Practice Learning for Disabled Social Work Students*, Southampton: SWAP.

Sayce, L. (2000) *From Psychiatric Patient to Citizen*, Basingstoke: Palgrave Macmillan.

Schorr, A. (1992) *The Personal Social Services: An Outside View*, York: Joseph Rowntree Foundation.

Scott, R. A. (1970) 'The Constructions and Conceptions of Stigma by Professional Experts', in J. Douglas (ed.) *Deviance and Respectability: The Social Construction of Moral Meanings*, New York: BASK Books.

Selfe, L. and Stow, L. (1981) *Children with Handicaps*, London: Hodder & Stoughton.

Shakespeare, T. (1996) 'Power and Prejudice: Issues of Gender, Sexuality and Disability', in L. Barton (ed.) *Disability & Society: Emerging Issues and Insights*, Harlow: Longman.

Shakespeare, T. (1997) 'Researching Disabled Sexuality', in C. Barnes and G. Mercer (eds), *Doing Disability Research*, Leeds: The Disability Press.

Shakespeare, T., Gillespie-Sells, K. and Davies, D. (1996) *The Sexual Politics of Disability: Untold Desires*, London: Cassell.

Shaping Our Lives (2010) A National Network of Service Users and Disabled People. www.shapingourlives.org.uk.

Shearer, A. (1981b) *Disability: Whose Handicap?*, Oxford: Blackwell.

Shearer, A. (1984) *Centres for Independent Living in the US and the UK – an American Viewpoint*, London: King's Fund Centre.

Silburn, R. (1983) 'Social Assistance and Social Welfare: the Legacy of the Poor Law', in P. Bean and S. MacPherson (eds) *Approaches to Welfare*, London: Routledge & Kegan Paul.

Social Services Inspectorate (1991a) *Care Management and Assessment: Managers Guide*, London: HMSO.

Social Services Inspectorate (1991b) *Care Management and Assessment: Practitioners Guide*, London: HMSO.

Southampton CIL (2010) *The 12 Basic Rights*. www.southamptoncil.co.uk/about/12-basic-rights/.

Southampton CIL (2011) Campaigning can't stop for Xmas http://southamptoncil.wordpress.com/category/disabled-people/.

Stevens, A. (1991) *Disability Issues*, London: CCETSW.

Stewart, J., Harris, J., and Sapey, B. (1999) 'Disability and Dependency: Origins and Futures of "Special Needs" Housing for Disabled People', *Disability and Society*, 14(1) pp. 5–20.

Stewart, W. (1979) *The Sexual Side of Handicap*, Cambridge: Woodhead-Faulkner.

Stuart, O. (1994) 'Journey from the Margin: Black Disabled People and the Antiracist Debate', in N. Begum, M. Hill and A. Stevens (eds) *Reflections: The Views of Black Disabled People on their Lives and on Community Care*, London: CCETSW.

Swain, J. (1981) *Adopting a Life-Style*, Milton Keynes: Open University Press.

Swain, J., Finkelstein, V., French, S. and Oliver, M. (eds) (1993) *Disabling Barriers: Enabling Environments*, London: Sage.

Tate, D. G., Maynard, F. and Forchheimer, M. (1992) 'Evaluation of a Medical Rehabilitation and Independent Living Programme for Persons with Spinal Cord Injury', *Journal of Rehabilitation*, 58, pp. 25–8.

Taylor, D. (1977) *Physical Impairment Social Handicap*, London: Office of Health Economics.

Tepper, M. (1999) 'Letting go of Restrictive Notions of Manhood: Male Sexuality, Disability and Chronic Illness', *Sexuality and Disability*, 17(1) pp. 36–52.

The Poverty Site (2011) 'Work and Disability', www.poverty.org.uk/45/index.shtml?2.

Think Local, Act Personal (2011) *Think Local, Act Personal – a sector-wide commitment to moving forward with personalisation and community-based support*, January 2011.

Thomas, C. (1999) *Female Forms: Experiencing and Understanding Disability*, Buckingham: Open University Press.

Thomas, C. (2004) 'How is Disability Understood? An Examination of Sociological Approaches', *Disability & Society*, 19(6) pp. 569–83.

Thomas, C. (2007) *Sociologies of Disability and Illness – Contested Ideas in Disability Studies and Medical Sociology*, Basingstoke: Palgrave Macmillan.

Thomas, P. (2004) 'The Experience of Disabled People as Customers in the Owner Occupation Market', *Housing Studies*, 19(5) pp. 781–94.

Thomas, P. (2011) '"Mate Crime": Ridicule, Hostility and Targeted Attacks against Disabled People', *Disability and Society*, 26(1) pp. 107–11.

Thomas, P. and Clark, L. (2010a) *Building Positive Partnerships: An agreement between Family Carer's Organisations, Disabled People's Organisations, Deaf People's Organisations and User Led Organisations*, Manchester: Breakthrough UK.

Thomas, P. and Clark, L. (2010b) *Consultation on Liverpool's Short Break Provision*, Accrington: North West Training and Development Team.

Thomas, P. and Ormerod, M. (2005) 'Adapting to Life – are adaptations a remedy for disability?', in M. Foord and P. Simic (eds) *Housing and Community Care and Supported Housing – Resolving Contradictions*, London: Chartered Institute of Housing.

Thompson, N. (1993) *Anti-Discriminatory Practice*, Basingstoke: Macmillan.

Thompson, N. (1998) *Promoting Equality*, Basingstoke: Macmillan.

Thompson, N. (2001) *Anti-Discriminatory Practice*, 3rd edn, Basingstoke: Macmillan.

Thompson, N. (2002) 'Social Movements, Social Justice and Social Work', *British Journal of Social Work*, 32, 711–22.

Tomlinson, S. (1982) *The Sociology of Special Education*, London: Routledge & Kegan Paul.

Topliss, E. (1979) *Provision for the Disabled*, 2nd edn, Oxford: Blackwell, with Martin Robertson.

Townsend, P. (1979) *Poverty in the United Kingdom*, Harmondsworth: Penguin.

Toynbee, P. (2008) 'The Beginning of the End of a Cruel, Impractical Edict', www.guardian.co.uk/commentisfree/2008/dec/13/assisted-suicide-law-polly-toynbee.

Trieschmann, R. B. (1980) *Spinal Cord Injuries*, Oxford: Pergamon Press.

Union of Physically Impaired Against Segregation (UPIAS) (1975) Policy Statement, London: Union of Physically Impaired Against Segregation. http://www.leeds.ac.uk/disability-studies/archiveuk/UPIAS/UPIAS.pdf.

Union of Physically Impaired Against Segregation (UPIAS) and Disability Alliance (1976a) *Fundamental Principles of Disability*, London: Union of Physically Impaired Against Segregation. www.leeds.ac.uk/disability-studies/archiveuk/UPIAS/fundamental principles.pdf.

United Nations (on line) Convention on the Rights of Persons with Disabilities http://www.un.org/disabilities/convention/conventionfull.shtml.

United Nations (undated) Convention on the Rights of Persons with Disabilities and Optional Protocol. www.un.org/disabilities/documents/convention/convoptprot-e.pdf.

Üstün, T. B., Kostanjsek, N., Chatterji, S. and Rehm, J. (2010) *Measuring Health and Disability Manual for WHO Disability Assessment Schedule WHODAS 2.0*, Geneva: World Health Organization. http://whqlibdoc.who.int/publications/2010/9789241547598_eng.pdf.

Wates, M. (2002) *Supporting Disabled Adults in their Parenting Role*, York: Joseph Rowntree Foundation.

Wates, M. (2004) 'Righting the Picture: Disability and Family Life' in J. Swain, S. French, C. Barnes and C. Thomas (eds) *Disabling Barriers – Enabling Environments*, 2nd edn, London: Sage.

Watson, L., Tarpey, M., Alexander, K. and Humphreys, C. (2003) *Supporting People: Real change? Planning housing and support for marginal groups*, York: Joseph Rowntree Foundation.

Weller, D. J. and Miller, P. M. (1977) 'Emotional Reactions of Patient, Family, and Staff in Acute Care Period of Spinal Cord Injury: Part 2', *Social Work in Health Care*, 3.

Welshman, J. (2004) 'The Unknown Times', *Journal of Social Policy*, 33(2) pp. 225–47.

Westcott, H. (1993) *Abuse of Children and Adults with Disabilities*, London: NSPCC.

Westcott, H. and Cross, M. (1995) *This Far and No Further: Towards Ending the Abuse of Disabled Children*, Birmingham: Venture Press.

Wilding, P. (1982) *Professional Power and Social Welfare*, London: Routledge & Kegan Paul.

Willis, M. (1995) 'Customer Expectations of Service Quality at Community Team Offices', *Social Services Research*, 4, pp. 57–67.

World Health Organization (2002) *Towards a Common Language for Functioning, Disability and Health: ICF*, Geneva: World Health Organization.

World Health Organization (2010) WHODAS-2, Geneva: World Health Organization.

Zarb, G. (1991) 'Creating a Supportive Environment: Meeting the Needs of People who are Ageing with a Disability', in M. Oliver (ed.) *Social Work, Disabled People and Disabling Environments*, London: Jessica Kingsley.

Zarb, G. (1993) 'The dual experience of ageing with a disability', in J. Swain, V. Finkelstein, S. French and M. Oliver (eds.) *Disabling Barriers – Enabling Environments*, London: Sage.

Zarb, G. and Nadash, P. (1994) *Cashing in on Independence*, London: Policy Studies Institute for the British Council of Disabled People.

Zarb, G., Oliver, M. and Silver, J. (1990) *Ageing with Spinal Cord Injury: the Right to a Supportive Environment?*, London: Thames Polytechnic/Spinal Injuries Association.

Index